MW01503203

Why Trump?

Why Some People Support Him—
How the Rest of Us Can Respond

Douglas Giles

Also by Douglas Giles

Left Wing, Right Wing, People, and Power:
The Core Dynamics of Political Action

How We Are and How We Got Here:
A Practical History of Western Philosophy

Individuals in the Social Lifeworld:
A Social Philosophy of Heidegger's Dasein

Rethinking Misrecognition and Struggles for Recognition:
Critical Theory Beyond Honneth

ISBN: 978-1-7358808-9-1

Real Clear Philosophy

Contents

1. Framing the Issue: What Is the Issue?

Many people talk about Donald Trump. Some people love him, and some people hate him. Some people try to explain why people love or hate Trump. Despite the copious conversation and plenteous explanations, there's a lack of clarity about why people support Trump. Neither academia nor the political pundits can adequately explain the phenomenon that is Trump.

Regardless of how you feel about Trump, the fact remains that he wins. He won the 2016 election fair and square. Yes, he lost the 2020 election fair and square, but he turned that into a win, as evidenced by the unquestioning devotion he still receives from a segment of the US population. Trump still possesses considerable social power.

Why Trump? Why do some people support him? Why has the subject of Trump become the dominant subject of US politics? I will consider those questions, and connected questions, and attempt to answer them in a constructive manner.

But what if I told you that the subject of these questions isn't Trump? It isn't, not really. Realizing that simple reality opens the door to a deeper understanding of the particular strain of US political culture that is behind the movement that currently takes Trump as its center of focus. There is little new in Trump or the things he says and does. His success in attaining power lies in his ability to harness a long-simmering feeling in a segment of the American population.

It's Not About Trump

When I began conducting research for this book, I did a search for "Trump" in my far-too-large collection of saved e-mails. The oldest e-mail I still have that mentioned Trump is this one from 2011:

MAY 16, 2011

Comedians Beg Trump to Reconsider
20,000 Jokers March on Trump Tower

NEW YORK (The Borowitz Report) – Distraught at the news that Donald Trump will not seek the Republican nomination for President, the nation's comedians took to the streets today, begging Mr. Trump to reconsider.

The largest gathering of comedians took place in Mr. Trump's hometown of Manhattan, where an estimated crowd of 400,000 jokers marched on Trump Tower.

"I for one am devastated that Donald Trump has decided not to throw his hair in the ring," said Jackie LaRossi, a comedian who is a regular at Manhattan's Chuckle Barrel comedy club.

Shelley Schwartzenbaum, who headlines at the Komedy Kantina in Teaneck, New Jersey, added, "I guess he wanted to spend more time with the family of ferrets who nest on his head."

A huge roar came up from the crowd when Mr. Trump made a brief appearance, reassuring the comedians that he would continue to be a laughingstock in the private sector.

Comedian Andy Borowitz's satirical e-mail newsletter, The Borowitz Report, reminds us that as early as 2011, Trump was both mulling a run for president and was the butt of ridicule.

Trump didn't run in 2012 but did in 2016. Initially, his run for the presidency was dismissed either as a joke or as the road to an extremism so unpalatable and unthinkable that it couldn't possibly succeed. Few thought he would win the election, including the Hillary Clinton campaign, which helped to elevate Trump's profile early in the primary race, believing him to be the potential Republican nominee most beatable as a general election candidate.[1] Clinton and her team were

---

[1] Gabriel Debenedetti, "They Always Wanted Trump," *Politico Magazine*,

correct in labeling Trump as a "Pied Piper candidate" but wrong in believing that he would lead the Republicans to electoral defeat.

But this book is not another inside-the-Beltway rehash of electoral politics. Nor is it another retrospective on what Trump has said and done. This book is neither a hit piece against Trump nor a hagiography extolling Trump. This book is about the United States and its unique strain of right-wing politics. Love him or hate him, Trump is a product of America—and here's the important thing: Trump is a symptom far more than he is a cause.

Yes, we are witnessing a right-wing movement that centers itself on Trump, but this movement isn't about Trump. He is a focal point, but there is much more going on here. Casting the movement as being led by Trump mischaracterizes not only the movement but also the nature of American culture and politics.

In this book, I will try to clarify this mischaracterization by asking a simple question: Why do some people follow Trump? They have a movement; they call it "MAGA." Yes, the Trump campaign team pushes the slogan "make America great again," but their marketing was more reaction than innovation. The 1980 presidential campaign of Ronald Reagan invented the "make America great again" slogan.[2]

Crucial to understanding Trump's appeal is to realize that there is little new in Trump's message. Technology, particularly social media, sharpens and intensifies the message, but its contents, and the feelings behind it, are nearly as old as the United States.

November 07, 2016.
https://www.politico.com/magazine/story/2016/11/hillary-clinton-2016-donald-trump-214428/.

[2] Robert E. Matthews, Jr., "Button, Ronald Reagan, 1980," *The Smithsonian Institution*, accessed June 7, 2024, https://www.si.edu/object/button-ronald-reagan-1980%3Anmah_522618.

The Need to Dig Deeper

It is common in the media to attribute support for Trump to disaffected whites.[3] This well-worn trope has a grain of truth to it and has the appeal of simplicity, but it is a judgment that is vague and inadequate. To say those who support Trump because they are "disaffected whites" is contemptuous and unproductive. It dismisses the complexities of social life and real people who possess real power. Why do some people feel that Trump is a solution to the problems they feel are present in America?

The issue isn't Trump. The issue is that reservoir of American feeling that he has managed to tap into and exploit. The issue is what has come out of the shadows and into the mainstream—a strain of reactionism that is unique to the United States, deriving from the country's unique history.

If you want to say that Trump is a wannabe strongman or authoritarian, you have good grounds for such an argument. But more important than such an argument is solving the riddle of why some people want a strongman as head of an authoritarian government.

Politics is about power. Anyone can want power, but no one can gain political power alone. Trump was fairly elected in 2016 by people who wanted him to become president, many of whom now want him again to become president. Why Trump? The power resides in those people more than in Trump. Who are the people in the MAGA movement? What are their concerns?

What are people in the MAGA movement hoping for? What do they feel would make America great? Those who support Trump frequently say they are living under tyranny in America. What do they mean? Why do they imagine that a

---

[3] Clarence Page, "Why Donald Trump appeals to disaffected white voters," *Chicago Tribune*, November 10, 2015, https://www.chicagotribune.com/2015/11/10/why-donald-trump-appeals-to-disaffected-white-voters/.

better alternative is an authoritarian government that would be even more tyrannical? Is it because they believe they would not be the target of the tyranny? Would they be correct?

We need also to ask if people in the MAGA movement are really willing to resort to violence. The January 6, 2021, attack on the United States Capitol Building in Washington, DC, has become so much a political football between the two major parties that the significance and implications of the attack have been lost. Was it an aberration? Or a prelude? Today, some Trump supporters say they see bloodshed as necessary.[4] Talk is cheap; do they intend to follow up their words with actions?

We need to dig deeper, beneath the simplistic dismissals, jokes, and talking points, and ask questions. The issue isn't Trump. The issue is much larger, deeper, and older. Let's dive in.

---

[4] Rachel Leingang, "'No Way Out without Bloodshed': The Right Believe the US Is under Threat and Are Mobilizing," *The Guardian*, June 2, 2024, https://www.theguardian.com/us-news/article/2024/jun/02/far-right-mobilizing-biden-presidency.

2. If You Think Trump Is the Problem. . .

The corporate media outlets sell their political coverage as a play-by-play of a sports game. One side is winning, one side is losing, come watch the spectacle. The media talking heads, or "pundits" as they are sometimes called, opine on who is scoring more points against the other in the messaging battle. Granted, elections do decide a winner and the losers, but there is far more to politics than elections, and politics is not a game.

What the corporate media loves is conflict. To receive any coverage from the media, politicians and their spokespeople know they need to provide sound bites, the edgier and more contentious the better. Politics is played out on television, a war of words among politicians grasping for sound bites and hoping for replays on the news and talk shows.

The biggest casualties in the made-for-TV sound bite contest are the issues. Serious, in-depth discussion of serious, complex issues can't be reduced to quick sound bites. Thus, the corporate media news programs aren't much interested in discussion of issues. The two political parties of the US party duopoly are quite happy to feed the media's politics-as-sports narrative because coming up with edgier quips is much easier than thinking about policy positions.

A politician's easiest way to make up an edgy sound bite for the media to amplify is to smear the political opposition. "The other side is the problem," is the politicians' answer to most questions. The media wants conflict, and the political parties are happy to provide it. The media engages in little analysis of actual political issues or how those issues affect people, so why should politicians?

The political sniping that dominates America these days is not only nonproductive but also actively harmful. No one benefits from childish memes attacking Trump and his allies or Biden and his allies. Nevertheless, such attacks are just about all that we hear anymore, including from politicians. America isn't solving its problems because the leaders are more interested in blaming their opponents than in working to solve problems. The media loves the mudslinging and sniping, but it doesn't help address the issues or solve problems. I'm not interested in this blame game beyond pointing it out.

Is Trump the Problem?

What I am interested in is digging into the question of why people support Trump. Democrats tell us that Trump is the problem; and yes, Trump and Republicans say that Democrats are the problem, but simply repeating back the mudslinging just repeats the vicious cycle.

Is Trump the problem with American politics? Let's take a quick quiz.
1. Is Trump a liar?
2. Is Trump a greedy self-absorbed businessman?
3. Does Trump live in a privileged bubble detached from reality?

If you answered "yes" to these three questions, you are correct.

Okay, now let's take a second quiz.
1. Is Trump the first politician to lie?
2. Is Trump the first greedy self-absorbed businessman?
3. Is Trump the first to live in a privileged bubble detached from reality?

If you answered "no" to these three questions, you are correct.

The purpose of this brief exercise is to steer the conversation away from Trump to the much more useful topic of the social system that created Trump and enabled him to become president. Trump is a symptom of a much larger set of problems.

You may respond, "but Trump is exceptional!" Yes, but only in being exceptionally open and blatant about what he is. Consider the possibility that Trump is no more and no less than a somewhat more dishonest, self-absorbed, oblivious politico who has a whole lot less impulse control. Consider also the possibility that he is a politician in the right place at the right time saying the right things.

What Is the Problem?

How is it that this particular deeply dishonest, self-absorbed, and oblivious politico was able to become president? That Trump was elected president of the United States in 2016 and could very well win reelection in 2024 is less a statement about Trump than it is about the United States. How this has happened and what it means need to be considered.

Trump became president within a system. He's responsible for his actions, but it is a system that allowed, if not enabled, him to gain power. If Trump is wrong, then something is also wrong with the American system that is enabling his wrongdoing.

Because here's the thing: All of the problems that are today plaguing the United States were there before Trump, and they've been there a long time. Trump didn't create any of them; he simply is more shameless about exacerbating and exploiting them.

What are the accusations made against Trump and his presidency? What, if anything, is new in them? Let's address a list of some of the most frequently made accusations against Trump.

- Racism? United States has had that since its inception. Remember that the Constitution enshrined Blacks as three-fifths of a person[5] but gave them zero-fifths of voting rights.

- Sexism? Also ever present.
- Hostility toward immigrants? The paradox is the United States is a nation of immigrants, but each group of immigrants was hostile toward the next ones. (I'll talk more about that in a latter chapter.)
- Neglect of the environment? Nixon created the Environmental Protection Agency over 50 years ago for a reason.[6]
- Corruption? Power corrupts; look at Nixon. It has corrupted US presidents and administrations—nearly every single one in US history.[7]
- Alienating foreign nations? Isolationism has dominated American foreign policy from the country's inception.[8]
- Denial of science? There's a long history of that from US presidents.[9]
- Hostility toward the working poor? You can't possibly believe that's new.
- Social media misbehavior? Okay, I'll give you that one, but imagine if Nixon or Reagan had had a Twitter (X) account.

---

[5] "The Constitution of the United States: A Transcription," *National Archives and Records Administration*, November 4, 2015, https://www.archives.gov/founding-docs/constitution-transcript, Article 1, Section 2, Clause 3.

[6] United States Environmental Protection Agency, "The Origins of EPA," accessed June 7, 2024, https://www.epa.gov/history/origins-epa.

[7] For a long list of political scandals in all three branches of the US federal government with a plethora of references (936 as if this writing) see, "List of Federal Political Scandals in the United States," accessed June 7, 2024, https://en.wikipedia.org/wiki/List_of_federal_political_scandals_in_the_United_States.

[8] Council on Foreign Relations, "Excerpt: Isolationism—An Anatomy of Isolationism," accessed June 7, 2024, https://www.cfr.org/excerpt-isolationism.

[9] Matthew Dallek, "The GOP Has a Long History of Ignoring Science. Trump Turned It into Policy," *Washington Post,* October 9, 2020, https://www.washingtonpost.com/outlook/the-gop-has-a-long-history-of-ignoring-science-trump-turned-it-into-policy/2020/10/09/53574602-0917-11eb-859b-f9c27abe638d_story.html.

The point is that if you are honest and not blinded by partisanship, you have to admit that any wrongs of Donald Trump are manifestations of long-entrenched wrongs.

If you want to accuse Trump of being more egregious or extreme on any issue, you have good justifications, but recognize that he is being more extreme in behaviors long-present in US history. Trump is simply a symptom. It is better to treat causes than symptoms.

What is the solution to Trump's extremism? It's certainly not repeating back to them simplistic sloganeering, name-calling, and memes. I don't for a second suggest that we not oppose Trump's excesses, but unless you are also willing to oppose the wrongs that are historically entrenched in the United States' political and legal systems that enable Trump and the MAGA movement, you are, in the end, also enabling Trump—and future Trumps, who just might be worse.

We need to deal with causes more than with symptoms. Addressing the root causes of problems is the road to solving them. To recognize root causes, we need a clearer understanding of society and its history. On the question of why people support Trump, the answer requires some understanding of American history and much understanding of the dynamics of politics.

3. The Lessons of the Power Spectrum

Politics is complex. To make sense of anything political, we need to peel back that surface rhetoric and look at what's really going on. We can better understand the movement that currently centers itself on Trump by viewing it in the context of the political power spectrum.

In my book, *Left Wing, Right Wing, People, and Power*, I explained that the central dynamic of politics is the conflict over power. Despite specific differences of time and place, political actions consistently are efforts to preserve or change the structures of power and who possesses power.

I describe the power dynamic in this way:

> Every person lives within a social space shaped by social institutions and norms that directly and indirectly inform people as to what they are able and allowed to do. The structure of the social space has significant effects on individuals' efforts to express and act on their desires, which is why power is central to politics and social life. Individual people seek to express and expand their power in the social space around them so that they become able to express more and do more in their lives.[10]

The structure of power within a social space—a society or community—will have a greater or lesser concentration of power.

---

[10] Douglas Giles, *Left Wing, Right Wing, People, and Power: The Core Dynamics of Political Action* (Real Clear Philosophy, 2024), 15.

Central to a nation's politics is the structure of power relations and the shares of power among various groups. Regarding these dimensions of power, we can think of two end points on a spectrum of political power structures. One end point is a structure in which power in a society is concentrated into one person or small assembly of persons. The other end point is power uniformly shared among all groups and individuals within a society.[11]

The power spectrum is the political spectrum that is usually thought of in terms of the left wing and the right wing.

In broad terms, those on the right wing of the spectrum wish power to be more concentrated and limited to select people, and those on the left wing of the spectrum wish power to be more widely circulated and thus enjoyed by more people. The goal of the right wing is a more restricted hierarchical society, and the goal of the left wing is a society open to the participation of more people. The greater a society's social and political structures concentrate power, the more right-wing that society is. The more a society circulates power among its citizens, the more left-wing it is. The political spectrum is the spectrum of power concentration.

It's Not About Clichés

My colleagues in academia too often dismiss those who support Trump as uneducated hicks living in an upside down world of alternative facts, though to be fair, it was the Trump team that invented the term "alternative facts."[12] Still, we can't understand people by dismissing them, and condescension is

---

[11] Giles, *Left Wing, Right Wing*, 16.
[12] Kellyanne Conway, "Meet the Press" interview broadcast January 22, 2017, https://www.nbcnews.com/meet-the-press/video/conway-press-secretary-gave-alternative-facts-860142147643.

unhelpful. We have to listen to people, including and perhaps especially, those people with whom we disagree.

Saying that Trump and people who support him believe falsehoods is insufficient. When people believe falsehoods, we do well to uncover why. When people weaponize falsehoods, we need to understand what they are doing and why.

Another common dismissal of Trump and the MAGA movement is to label them as fascists. They are certainly right-wingers, but I agree with historian Jonathan Zatlin that critics of Trump bandy about the term "fascist" facilely and without historical reference. Fascism was a historical phenomenon of interwar Europe, Zatlin says, and you can't call Trump Republicans fascists, even though it's important to recognize that what they are saying is completely unoriginal.[13] Zatlin concurs that we need to understand Trump and his followers in the context of a particular strand of American politics that dates back to the country's founding.

Also unhelpful are the continual acts of name-calling and meme making by those in political opposition to Trump and Republicans. Insulting Trump and those who support him gives critics a short-lived sense of accomplishment, but it does nothing to shed light on the pro-Trump movement, much less resist it. Such immature behavior certainly does nothing to counter anything that Trump or the people who support him do or say.

Trump and MAGA embody a quintessential oppositional politics, but the Democratic Party has responded with its own oppositional politics. US politics has for eight years now been dominated by two parties each claiming the other party is the enemy of the United States itself. Meanwhile, few of America's problems are even addressed much less solved. This antagonistic form of politics is itself a significant problem.

---

[13] Rich Barlow, "Are Trump Republicans Fascists?" *BU Today*, February 11, 2022, https://www.bu.edu/articles/2022/are-trump-republicans-fascists/.

The Three Trajectories of the Right Wing

The right wing of the political spectrum historically evolved in three trajectories—conservatism, libertarianism, and reactionism.[14] They are at times starkly different, but they share a fundamental belief that society should be structured such that power is concentrated in a specific segment of society.

Conservatism as we know it today emerged in the 1790s as a reassertion that power should be held by the merchant class and the landowner class. Conservatives like Edmund Burke in Great Britain and the Federalists in the newly formed United States were pushing back against the French revolutionaries' radical demands to dismantle the traditional power structures of the French monarchy. To this day, the impetus of resisting change and reasserting traditional hierarchies continues to characterize the right wing.

Libertarianism arose in the late 1900s as a more extreme version of power concentration in the merchant class and the landowner class. Robert Nozick[15] provided arguably the strongest intellectual expression of libertarian ideology. Nozick advocated for the concept of a minimal state wherein there is minimal intervention from the state and people are entitled to economic and personal freedoms. However, since this "minarchist" state, as Nozick called it, would impose no oversight or regulations on business activities, the result would be a political structure in which the government exists only as a servant of the property interests of the wealthy.

Reactionism doesn't have a specific origin but is a political perspective that has long simmered in society. Reactionaries are people who approve of and seek to reaffirm previous hierarchical social divisions, but they don't possess the power of the upper class. They nevertheless perceive themselves as possessing some social privilege by dint of being

---

[14] Giles, *Left Wing, Right Wing*, 55–63.
[15] Robert Nozick, *Anarchy, State, and Utopia* (Blackwell, 1974).

the "right" ethnicity, religion, or other social identity that traditionally held a higher position in the power structure. Reactionism is a strong desire to resist social changes and reassert traditional hierarchies. As I previously wrote:

> Reactionism is the response to—and the reaction against—increased diversity and inclusion in society. Reactionaries feel they are under siege and even oppressed by changing social norms and demographic shifts. Not all people who are unsettled by social change take political action to oppose those changes. Those who do take action are the right-wing block that seeks to reassert traditional, even archaic, power relations and structures. These are the reactionaries, whose political focus is on reversing the long cultural trend of increasing diversity and inclusion that has circulated more power to more people.[16]

The drive to reverse social change and increased diversity is a key impetus of reactionism. Reactionism is the dread fear that somewhere someone you feel is your inferior is being recognized as your equal. Such a fear can be a strong motivator for political action.

Right-wing political movements are composed of various combinations of people from these three trajectories. Like all political movements, they are concerned with power, and being concerned with asserting concentrations of power, they are right wing.

Political Movements and the Power Spectrum

People who participate in politics, however they are involved and whether they are left wing or right wing, are all guided by a sense of what they believe is ethically good. People join political movements that they believe will act to improve

---

[16] Giles, *Left Wing, Right Wing*, 60–61.

their lives if not society at large. Both the left wing and the right wing seek increased prosperity and freedom but have different conceptions of how to achieve that.

Labeling political movements as "left wing" and "right wing" is independent of any ethical judgments about the proponents' intentions. All of these movements would see their particular causes as ethically just; they are seeking what is, in their opinion, the ethical good.

There are situations in which a greater concentration of power leads to better outcomes just as there are situations in which greater circulation of power lead to better outcomes. Sincere, intelligent discussions can—and should—be had about whether particular circumstances warrant a greater or lesser concentration of power.

The power spectrum manifests in a number of areas. Government can be centralized or devolved. Participation in government, such as access to electoral power, can be more or less restricted. Wealth and economic opportunities can be closely or widely held. Social status, rights, and freedoms can be granted to only certain groups of people or guaranteed more broadly across society.

In each area of society, when people and movements disagree, the central issue of contention is the level of power concentration—who has power and how much power? Politics is complex, but within the complexity is the basic reality that all political positions and political actions are based on ideas of what degree of concentration of power is best. Political conflict is usually the disagreement over the best level and arrangement of power concentration.

The MAGA Political Movement

MAGA is best understood as a movement that is struggling for recognition of their status and wishes. In a way, the MAGA movement is like the US civil rights movement that struggled for recognition, but MAGA's struggle is for a different set of social norms and a different power structure. The civil rights movement was left wing in its push to circulate power—increase access to power for more people. MAGA is right wing in its push to concentrate power in their social demographics and to wind back the social reforms that increased power to people previously left out of the political, economic, and social power structures.

People take political actions because they are motivated by what they believe to be the ethical good. We can't forget that reality, even in the face of the angry rhetoric and violent actions of a political movement. MAGA is a political movement that sees the ethical good to be a return to a particular dream of an America when they believe America was "great." It's fair to say that their memory of how America used to be is selective. What isn't debatable is that the people in MAGA believe a greater concentration of power will make America "great again."

Saying there is a need to "make America great again" is clearly predicated on the opinion that America currently isn't great. Trump is not shy about saying that America is in decline and even failing. He is more reluctant to give specifics or facts supporting his negative opinion about America.

That Trump and people who support him have a fiercely negative opinion about the United States is highly important. That negativity defines their movement. Like all political movements, MAGA is about power. In their case, it is about reclaiming power they fear they don't have.

They wrap their fear in the flag and talk about America's past greatness, but they are less clear about when they feel that America was great. They want to roll back the clock, but roll it back to when? Before civil rights? Before feminism? Before the New Deal? Before the abolition of slavery? These aren't unfair questions if Trump and people who support him want to be understood and their movement taken seriously.

What Trump and people who support him are willing to show us indicates that theirs is a reactionary political movement. Their focus is on reversing America's long cultural trend of increasing diversity and inclusion that has circulated more power to more people.

It is possible to make rational objections to social and legal changes that have increased the circulation of power in the United States. Some arguments made by conservatives are rational objections and are worthy of discussion. However, Trump and people who support him are, it must be said, not offering rational objections. They are reactionaries. They are not conservatives—a fact on which Trump[17] and some conservatives[18] agree.

What calls itself "MAGA" is a political movement seeking to change the United States. That is their right as long as they act within the law. But therein lies a key difference between MAGA and other political movements, even right-wing ones.

The MAGA movement is steeped in the myth of American revolutionism—the conviction that part of what makes America great is its battle against threatening tyrants. Theirs is a battle of good versus evil—a reactionary political movement motivated by particular conceptions of good and evil that I will discuss at length in Chapter 8. Thus, people in the MAGA movement are open to feeling that their actions answer to a higher ethical good than acting within the law or conventional norms.

Trump exploits the reactionaries' desire to regain and reassert their power. But why do they support him? Why have they created a personality cult around Trump as a savior of their version of America? Trump has gained support because

[17] *Newsweek*, "Donald Trump Admits He's Not a Conservative," March 11, 2024, https://www.newsweek.com/donald-trump-admits-he-isnt-conservative-cnbc-squawk-box-1877949.
[18] Alexander Bolton, "Former Speaker Ryan: 'Trump's not a conservative, he's an authoritarian narcissist,'" *The Hill*, December 13, 2023, https://thehill.com/homenews/house/4359176-former-speaker-ryan-trumps-not-a-conservative-hes-an-authoritarian-narcissist/.
The Daily Show, "June 3, 2024 – Rep. Ken Buck," https://www.cc.com/episodes/bse7mc/the-daily-show-june-3-2024-rep-ken-buck-season-29-ep-53.

he can tap into a specific emotion that is common among reactionaries, and he is able to play a role—like an actor on television—in the particularly American brand of that dramatic emotion. Again, there is little new in Trump or why some people support politicians like him.

4. The Strongest Power in Politics

Max Scheler (No, there are no photos of him in which he doesn't look grumpy, which apparently was not his personality at all)

Max Scheler (1874–1928) optimistically saw the possibilities for humanity if we could recognize the positive value of the individual person. Scheler was also able to see the negative possibilities of human interaction and identified a major motivator for social and political conflict that described much of the century to come.

In 1914, near the outbreak of what came to be known as World War I, Scheler wrote the short book *Ressentiment*.[19] With the concept of ressentiment (similar to but different from resentment), Scheler described the difference between actions from love that seek to improve others and actions from negative values that seek to diminish others. Scheler's concept of ressentiment can help us understand why people support Trump and why they take the political actions that they do.

Friedrich Nietzsche (1844–1900) also used the word "ressentiment" to describe the motivation behind what he called "slave morality."[20] However, his use of the concept was tied up in his own ressentiment against Christianity and his desire to diminish it. He essentially used the concept more as a rhetorical weapon than as a description of political action, equating the man of ressentiment with the man of the Judeo-Christian tradition. Nietzsche is helpful in his claim that

---

[19] Max Scheler, *Ressentiment* (Marquette University Press, 1994).
[20] Friedrich Nietzsche, *On the Genealogy of Morals*, ed. Kieth Ansell-Pearson, trans. Carol Diethe (Cambridge University Press, 2007).

ressentiment gives birth to new values in its conceiving of a dualism of the evil enemy—the evil against which one contrasts oneself as the good. That is true, as we shall see, but because Scheler applies the concept of ressentiment in a broader context, applicable to all of humankind, it is his discussion on which I will focus.

Ressentiment

According to Merriam-Webster, "ressentiment" is a word meaning "deep-seated resentment, frustration, and hostility accompanied by a sense of being powerless to express these feelings directly."[21] Scheler defined ressentiment this way:

> Ressentiment is an incurable, persistent feeling of hating and despising which occurs in certain individuals and groups. It takes its root in equally incurable "impotencies" or weaknesses that those subjects suffer from. . . . They can permeate a whole culture, era, and an entire moral system. The feeling of ressentiment leads to false moral judgements made on other people who are devoid of this feeling.[22]

Anyone paying attention can recognize that this describes much of the adversarial politics that the world has seen for generations.

But before you start pointing fingers, saying "yeah, that describes those people I disagree with," understand that Scheler makes several crucial distinctions about what constitutes ressentiment. He acknowledges the difference between objectively legitimate grievances and imagined ones and between true moral judgments and false ones. Those differences are reflected in individuals' intentions and goals.

---

[21] "Ressentiment." *Merriam-Webster.com Dictionary*, Merriam-Webster, accessed 16 June 2024, https://www.merriam-webster.com/dictionary/ressentiment.
[22] Scheler 45-46.

Ressentiment is different from the justified anger one feels when being mistreated. Ressentiment is a particular form of hatred that arises from beliefs that one is lacking recognition and thus is socially impotent. Struggles against real injustices are movements toward higher values such as justice, truth, and love that inspire positive actions. Acts motivated by ressentiment are movements toward lower values such as spite, vengeance, and malice that inspire negative actions.

Scheler states that ressentiment is a state in which one has lost a relation to positive values. This state triggers feelings of hopelessness and frustration that predispose one to regress to self-destructive indulgences or outward hostility to try to resolve the sense of impotence. The frustration and impotence characteristic of ressentiment are less a reaction to an actual external oppressor and more a self-inflicted sense of inadequacy over one's own real or imagined limitations.

The feelings of ressentiment lead to false moral judgments on others that Scheler calls "value delusions." These delusions are a form of moral blindness that results in "a tendency to belittle, degrade, dismiss or to 'reduce' genuine values as well as their bearers."[23] Individuals and groups in the psychological state of ressentiment are hampered in their ability to make sound moral judgments and tend to see values and other people through a filter of negative prejudice. Other people are made into surrogate enemies to compensate for a sense of impotency and are turned into targets for hostile judgments.

Ressentiment and the negative feelings it triggers become self-perpetuating. Even more, they become part of one's identity. The individual self-defines as cynical, aloof, and a judge of others, value delusions leading to arrogance, hubris, and double standards.

---

[23] Scheler 88.

Distilling Ressentiment

Scheler's concept of ressentiment is compelling and useful because it describes abstract and elastic psychological phenomena not restricted to a specific type of person or set of circumstances. Ressentiment describes both individuals and groups of people, including political movements. The concept does not describe all cases of personal or group political hostility, but it can help us to understand some, and perhaps many, social and political movements of the past 110 years.

In practice, the feelings of impotence and frustration in ressentiment instill envy and fear in people. A politician who can identify individuals' envies and fears, distill them further, direct them at a feasible target, and most effectively exploit them can win power. Plato understood this 2,400 years ago when he wrote about politics and the danger of a charismatic person gaining popular support and becoming a tyrant.[24] Many other things have changed since Plato, but the power of ressentiment and ressentiment as power have not.

Vladimir Lenin and the Bolsheviks distilled the ressentiment in the Russian population who were long oppressed by the czars and devasted by World War I. "We will protect you from the czarists and the capitalists," went the Bolshevik sales pitch. Lenin exploited fear and envy and violently gained power to become a new tyrant replacing the old tyrant.

It should never be forgotten that Adolf Hitler and the Nazi political party were elected by popular vote. Yes, they engaged in voter suppression and intimidation, but they won power because they effectively directed the ressentiment already present in people and directed it at a clear target. "We will protect you from the socialists, Bolsheviks, and Jews," the Nazis said, and they convinced enough people that the socialists and Bolsheviks were a threat to the Fatherland and

---

[24] Plato, *Republic*, Project Gutenberg, accessed June 23, 2024, http://www.gutenberg.org/ebooks/1497.

that the Nazi party would save them. Then the Nazis locked up all the socialists and Bolsheviks and repressed and murdered the Jews.

Once in power, as Frederic Jameson observed, the new ruling elite distills feelings of ressentiment to simultaneously justify their privileges and rationalize the denial of those same privileges to the poorer classes.[25] It's a pattern often repeated across history.

Ishaan Tharoor observes that the weaponizing of ressentiment is possibly the defining theme in global politics right now, [26] exploited by nationalists from Turkish President Recep Tayyip Erdoğan to French politician Marine Le Pen to former president Donald Trump.

Yes, in America, ressentiment is currently distilled and exploited by Trump. It usually works, so why not use it? Trump may not be the cleverest con man, but he isn't stupid. "I will protect you from the socialists and immigrants," Trump says.[27] Some people believe him and help him gain power.

The political exploitation of ressentiment is not restricted to Trump or politicians like him. It is a political strategy more than it is a political ideology. MAGA is one version of a movement motivated primarily by feelings of ressentiment. To further our understanding of the particular character of the MAGA movement, we can look at some specifics of how Trump exploits ressentiment.

---

[25] Frederic Jameson, *The Political Unconscious: Narrative as a Socially Symbolic Act* (Cornell University Press, 1981).

[26] Ishaan Tharoor, "What the World's Nationalists can Learn from Turkey and Erdogan," *Washington Post*, June 26, 2018, https://www.washingtonpost.com/news/worldviews/wp/2018/06/26/what-the-worlds-nationalists-can-learn-from-turkey-and-erdogan/.

[27] Sahlil Kapur, "Trump Revives Old Battle Cry Against 2020 Democrats: Socialism," *Bloomberg*, March 7, 2019, https://www.bloomberg.com/news/articles/2019-03-07/trump-revives-old-battle-cry-against-2020-democrats-socialism.

Two Cornerstones of Trump's Campaigns

Trump's exploitation of ressentiment focuses on distilling reactionaries' feelings of fear and weakness in the face of increasing diversity. He further focuses on harnessing their desire to reassert the traditional order—what Scheler would call a "value delusion"—their belief that the traditional power structure was for the greater good. Together these two focuses are the cornerstones of Trump's past and present campaigns and the political movement that focuses on him as a savior.

More than any single issue, anti-immigrant rhetoric was a major cornerstone of Trump's 2016 presidential campaign. He called for a "total and complete shutdown of Muslims entering the United States."[28] One of his first acts as president was an executive order with that effect.

Trump's heavy rhetoric about immigrants has escalated in the 2024 presidential campaign. His rhetoric exploits reactionaries' incurable, persistent feeling of hating and despising immigrants, Hispanic people in particular. In 2024, in the value delusions of Trump, there isn't immigration, there is a border invasion of rapists and murderers. "You will see horrible things [from immigrants] unless you elect me," Trump said on June 18, 2024,[29] weaponizing ressentiment and offering vague promises of protection.

Trump's rhetoric of ressentiment has extended beyond immigrants to Muslims, Blacks, feminists, liberals in general, the specter of "wokeness," and anyone he deems to be his opponents in government. On the one hand, these rhetorical targets express typical right-wing desires to concentrate power by denying it to others. On the other hand, these are assertions of value delusions intended to placate reactionaries'

---

[28] Jeremy Diamond, "Donald Trump: Ban all Muslim travel to U.S." *CNN*, December 7, 2015, https://www.cnn.com/2015/12/07/politics/donald-trump-muslim-ban-immigration/index.html.

[29] "WATCH LIVE: Trump attends presidential campaign rally in Racine, Wisconsin," *PBS News*, June 18, 2024, https://www.youtube.com/watch?v=X-XYXZXh-Hc.

fears of impotence in the face of social diversity and distill their ressentiment. Trump promises a government crackdown on immigrants, Muslims, Blacks, feminists, liberals, and so on because that is what the reactionaries desire, and that is why such rhetoric is one of the cornerstones of Trump's campaigns.

In another cornerstone of his 2016 campaign, Trump pledged to "drain the swamp" in Washington, DC, of corruption. He didn't invent the phrase "drain the swamp"—it had previously been used by a number of US politicians, most notably by Ronald Reagan.[30] In his use of the slogan, Trump was probably trying to latch on to the aura of Reagan among right-wingers.

It is debatable as to what steps the Trump administration took against corruption.[31] What isn't debatable is that a sizable number of Trump advisors and operatives were charged and convicted of crimes, some during his administration.[32]

Regardless of what Trump and his team did or didn't do, this was more than the usual hypocrisy of politicians. There's little doubt that the campaign rhetoric of "drain the swamp" was an appeal to ressentiment. The "swamp" to which Trump constantly referred was a dog whistle to the reactionary right that had little to do with ethics in government.

---

[30] Eric Garcia, "A History of 'Draining the Swamp,'" *Roll Call*, October 18, 2016, https://rollcall.com/2016/10/18/a-history-of-draining-the-swamp/.

[31] Josh Dawsey, Rosalind S. Helderman, and David A. Fahrenthold, "How Trump abandoned his pledge to 'drain the swamp,'" *Washington Post*, October 24, 2020, https://www.washingtonpost.com/politics/trump-drain-the-swamp/2020/10/24/52c7682c-0a5a-11eb-9be6-cf25fb429f1a_story.html.

[32] Soo Rin Kim, "Trump associates who have been sent to prison or faced criminal charges," *ABC News*, January 17, 2020, https://abcnews.go.com/Politics/trump-associates-prison-faced-criminal-charges/story?id=68358219.
Reuters. "What Trump allies have faced criminal charges?" *Reuters.com*, August 2, 2023, https://www.reuters.com/world/us/many-trumps-orbit-have-faced-criminal-charges-2023-02-16/.

The targets of Trump's rhetoric were alleged elitists in government—"liberals" and Democratic Party politicians. Trump labeled them as "corrupt" without alleging specific crimes. For Trump and those who support him, "corruption" in politics isn't about criminal activity, as Jason Stanley explains. "Corruption, to the fascist politician, is really about corruption of purity rather than of the law."[33] Stanley labels Trump a fascist, a label, which, as mentioned earlier, is not entirely applicable. Stanley's point remains, though, that for right-wingers, corruption isn't about ethical standards in government—bribery, graft, respect for the rule of law, and so on—corruption is about political ideology and cultural purity.

Corruption is in the eye of the beholder, and partisans in any political party are likely to believe that the other party is more corrupt than their own.[34] There is, nevertheless, a distinct character to Trump's use of allegations of corruption, and it connects with the rhetoric to distill ressentiment and fear of diversity.

Within the value delusions of the reactionaries, moral virtue is a question of whether another person shares their ressentiment-fueled hatred of certain people. Stanley is correct that the right wing seeks a return to a moral purity that they imagine existed back when America was "great." The core of that idea of purity is the traditional order—the traditional hierarchies of power in which foreigners, minorities, women, and others knew their place and were sharply reminded if they stepped outside of their place.

Those reactionaries who despise, for example, immigrants will feel that politicians who don't share those feelings are morally corrupt. Trump's rhetoric displays hatred

---

[33] Jason Stanley, *How Fascism Works: The Politics of Us and Them* (Random House, 2018), 36.

[34] Philip Bump, "Democrats and Republicans are Equally Likely to Say the Other Party's Candidate Is 'Too Corrupt,'" *The Washington Post*, March 15, 2024. https://www.washingtonpost.com/politics/2024/03/15/biden-trump-corrupt-poll/.

for immigrants, and that connects with reactionaries' feelings, so he is not corrupt.

This sounds simplistic—because it is. This is about ressentiment, not facts or reason. This political dynamic is not party partisanship, not Democrats versus Republicans. It is more base than that. We can see this in the hostile reactions by those in the MAGA movement to those Republicans who criticized the January 6 attack on the US Capitol building, forcing most of them eventually to give tacit approval to the violence.[35]

Whether Trump is responsible for the January 6 attack is up for debate. What's crucially important is that the world can't openly have such a debate. The value delusions of Trump and those who support him have redefined corruption as the divergence from the traditional order of the power structure. This explains why the Republican Party censured members of their own party willing to engage in legitimate debate about the January 6 attack.[36]

This redefinition of corruption also explains why the January 6 attack was less about allegiance to Trump and more about restoring a right-wing vision of order against the legal realities of a fair election and the constitutional process of certifying that election's results. To people who support Trump, he embodies a defense of the traditional order, the traditional hierarchies of power. Trump's corruption isn't the problem to them. They believe he's the solution. To them, subverting the constitutional process is morally defensible,

---

[35] PBS News, "One Year Ago, Republicans Condemned Jan. 6 Insurrection. Yesterday, Their Response Was Far More Muted," January 7, 2022, https://www.pbs.org/newshour/politics/one-year-ago-republicans-condemned-jan-6-insurrection-yesterday-their-response-was-far-more-muted.

[36] Alana Wise, "RNC votes to censure Reps. Liz Cheney and Adam Kinzinger over work with Jan. 6 panel," *NPR*, February 4, 2022, https://www.npr.org/2022/02/04/1078316505/rnc-censure-liz-cheney-adam-kinzinger-jan-6-committee-capitol.

and Congress upholding the Constitution is morally deplorable.

In 2016, Trump said that he could shoot someone in public and he wouldn't lose any votes.[37] The blasé reactions to his indictments and felony convictions from those who support him demonstrate that Trump wasn't wrong in saying this. Trump gains and retains people to support him because he knows how to distill and exploit the fears of a particular segment of the population. He effectively harnesses the ressentiment of the reactionary Right and turn it into a political machine of ressentiment.

---

[37] Colin Dwyer, "Donald Trump: 'I Could ... Shoot Somebody, and I Wouldn't Lose Any Voters,'" NPR, January 23, 2016. https://www.npr.org/sections/thetwo-way/2016/01/23/464129029/donald-trump-i-could-shoot-somebody-and-i-wouldnt-lose-any-voters.

5. People Aren't Stupid—They're Lazy Thinkers

Why does exploiting ressentiment work? Why can it be a successful strategy for any politician? I argue that it has much to do with a common aspect of human nature.

It is not uncommon for people opposed to the MAGA movement to degrade those who support Trump. We have all heard the rhetoric from Democrats that MAGA people are ignorant, uneducated, or stupid. Granted, MAGA people often say that Democrats are ignorant, uneducated, or stupid. We need to reject this childish pissing match and grapple with the bad psychological habit of which partisans of both parties are guilty. To be honest, we are all guilty of this at times.

People are smart. We call ourselves *Homo sapiens* for a reason. People are smart enough to figure out how to go to the moon. So why do a small minority of people choose to believe conspiracy theories such as the idea that we didn't go to the moon, or clearly false beliefs like that the Earth is flat, that vaccines don't work, that everything they disagree with (like election results) is false, and so on?

There are political motivations behind such false beliefs to be sure, the nature of which I will discuss in the next chapter on conspiracy theories. Mostly, though, people believe falsehoods not because they are stupid but because they are lazy. We normally think of people being lazy in the physical sense—being too lazy to get up and do something. People have physical capabilities that they choose to be too lazy to use, but people also have mental capabilities that they choose to be too lazy to use. Lazy thinking is a problem that is all too common, especially in politics.

Two Forms of Thinking

In philosophy, we talk a lot about the importance of critical thinking. We are thinking well when we avoid precipitancy and allow the world to show us what is the case while maintaining a critical view of what we are experiencing. We are thinking poorly when we rush to conclusions and are closed to new information. Good thinking is a deliberate, time-consuming effort. Poor thinking is being lazy—caring more about having an answer than having a correct answer.

Psychologist Daniel Kahneman, in his book, *Thinking, Fast and Slow*,[38] theorizes that people form thoughts in two ways. One is fast, automatic, and stereotypical thinking, and the second is slow, effortful, conscious thinking. Each way of thinking is appropriate for particular circumstances. We don't need to engage in effortful calculations to read a simple sentence or solve 2+2=x. Kahneman's argument is that human cognitive biases stem from people taking the mental shortcuts of automatic and stereotypical thinking when they would get better results by engaging with effortful, conscious thinking.

The forms of thinking that Dr. Kahneman identifies are a clinical version of a reality that philosophers have explored for centuries. Both forms of thinking are ways we all respond to the world, and we do need both forms. When interacting with the world around them, people can, and usually do, have simple, immediate reactions, but people can also respond with deliberate, thoughtful responses, though people act this way less often.

Philosopher William James acknowledged the usefulness of making fast decisions, meaning that sometimes circumstances require us to make a decision quickly.[39] For example, if a vehicle is speeding toward us, we don't wait to collect and think through all contingencies and possibilities for action—we quickly get out of the way.

Although James accepted the need for fast thinking, he preferred that we all spend the time and effort to think deliberately. He said that our thinking should be based on solid empirical evidence with an eye toward crafting beliefs

---

[38] Daniel Kahneman, *Thinking, Fast and Slow* (Farrar, Straus and Giroux, 2011).

[39] William James, *The Meaning of Truth* (Flame Tree 451, 2024).

that have value to us. The truth of an idea is its pragmatic usefulness, he argued. We are more likely to craft useful beliefs by assessing all available evidence and adjusting our beliefs to the facts.

James is correct that we believe all of our beliefs and consider them to be truths because we find them useful. He is also correct that usefulness is the goal of good-quality, deliberate, slow thinking. After all, what is the point of spending time and effort on thinking other than to arrive at answers that we can then use to accomplish our goals?

The key to James's pragmatism is that our thoughts need to connect with how things are in the world. Slow, deliberate thinking is philosophical thinking. It is the method by which we craft answers and solutions that reflect how things are in the world, adapt our thinking to the world, and fulfill our needs to create practically useful beliefs.

Lazy Thinking

James's realization that the truth of an idea lies in its usefulness makes a great deal of sense, but it also has a potential drawback. The problem is that lazy thinking is also useful. It's less useful, of course, because laziness is a motivation to settle for less. People settle for less when they believe it useful for them to do so.

People choose to be lazy because they get something out of it. Physical laziness is generally either a lack of caring or a way to try to get someone else to do something. Lazy thinking is likewise either an absence of care or a surrendering to others of the acts of finding answers and solutions.

Lazy thinkers are either apathetic or wanting someone else to do the thinking for them. Either way, lazy thinking is an evasion of one's personal responsibility to think and act for oneself. To fail to engage in deliberate thinking is an ethical failing.

The worst consequence of lazy thinking is that it severs beliefs from engagement with the world. Good thinking is a deliberate, time-consuming effort of practical engagement with the world, continually adjusting one's beliefs to one's experiences. It is that slow process of continual adjustment that keeps beliefs grounded and useful. Without the effort of that process, beliefs become less valuable over time because they lose connections with how the world is.

If you own a machine, like an automobile, and do not maintain it, the machine will eventually break down. Beliefs are the same. They must be maintained through continual, diligent effort and attention.

Lazy automobile owners end up with a broken automobile. Lazy thinkers end up with broken beliefs. Neither a broken automobile nor a broken belief has much value because they aren't useful.

People who fall into lazy thinking are evading their personal responsibility. They are letting other people do their thinking for them and are being too lazy to look at how things are in the world. Spending the effort to think through the claims of a conspiracy theory would dispel belief in that theory's false claims.

The tendency we all have for lazy thinking explains why exploiting ressentiment works. The strong, simplistic answers of emotional rhetoric can appeal to the bad psychological habit of lazy thinking. Skillful rhetoric provides people with fast, easy beliefs, beliefs that are useful to the believer when they reinforce false moral judgments of value delusions. When Trump says there is a border invasion of rapists and murderers, he is reinforcing their value delusions of people feeling ressentiment, and thus they find these simple but false moral judgments useful. They allow him to do their thinking for them. Fast and easy.

The temptation to be lazy in one's thinking is not restricted to reactionaries or to political action. We see lazy thinking in all areas of life and from all demographics. We see it in Democrats, who regurgitate rhetoric and memes containing false moral judgments as eagerly as Trump supporters do. People from all walks of life are willing to refuse to accept truths that are contrary to their desires. It's easier to deny facts than to have to think about how to adjust one's thinking to deal with those facts. Lazy thinking. Fast and easy.

It is incumbent upon everyone to engage in deliberate thinking despite it being slow and effortful. We owe it to ourselves and to everyone else. Lazy thinking is a temptation, and it is easy to justify falling into it. Just as it's easier to destroy than to create, it's easier to avoid one's responsibility and, so to speak, burn down the evidence all around and accept stupid and wrong beliefs. How many of society's problems stem from lazy thinking?

But we can't summarize support for Trump as lazy thinking alone. As mentioned, lazy thinking is a common habit that transcends political boundaries. Ressentiment is also a factor, but there are others. We can uncover one of those factors by looking at the question of why people believe conspiracy theories. We turn next to that question not only because Trump's rhetoric includes multiple conspiracy theories but also because the phenomena of conspiracy theories reveal some important features of the MAGA movement.

6. What Lurks Behind Conspiracy Theories?

Trump is not the leader of a movement but is a focal point for one. Trump is not a leader, but he is an artist—a particular type of artist. That's why we need to discuss conspiracy theories. Conspiracy theories play a significant role in forming movements like the one currently taking Trump as its focus.

Some people, despite all proof to the contrary, believe the moon landings were faked. Some people, despite all proof to the contrary, believe the last election was stolen. And those are just two of the many conspiracy theories that are believed by untold numbers of people.

How can we understand the phenomena of conspiracy theories? The idea of conspiracy theories conjures up stories about grassy knolls, UFO cover-ups, the Illuminati, and other wild ideas that most people consider to be nonsense. The people who believe them aren't all asylum inmates wearing tinfoil hats in fear of government mind control. Conspiracy theories are part of human culture. We cannot just dismiss them, if for no other reason than that we can't ignore the damage caused by belief in conspiracy theories. Recently, we saw the deaths of many people who believed conspiracy theories about the COVID-19 pandemic.

To ignore or ridicule beliefs in conspiracy theories is to be as dismissively arrogant as the conspiracy theory believers are about beliefs other than their own. We don't have to agree with the conspiracy theories, but we need to understand what they are, why some people believe them, and what lurks beneath them.

This chapter will discuss the philosophy of conspiracy theories, addressing the questions of what they are, why people believe them, how they function in social and political life, as well as their effect on society. Answering these questions will help explain why some people support Trump because the social dynamic of conspiracy theories overlaps with and supports movements like MAGA.

What Are Conspiracy Theories?

What are conspiracy theories, and why are they so common? First, we need to define what we are analyzing. I will define a conspiracy theory as follows:

A claim that you have figured out a powerful secret that "normal" people have not.

There are three components of this definition. One: Conspiracy theories are stories about secret cabals secretly meeting in secret places to secretly concoct secret plans. And yes, I stress the secret aspect of these stories. For a story to appeal to those who believe in conspiracy theories, it has to be about a deep, **dark** secret. By definition, a conspiracy is a secretive plot, but a conspiracy *theory* is about some seriously hidden, seriously **dark** skullduggery that is allegedly being brought to light.

Two: A conspiracy theory is a truth claim. This fact is often ignored but is especially important. People believe a conspiracy theory *because* they believe it is true. No matter how weird beliefs might be, every idea we hold to be true is a belief we feel we are justified in having. It is no different for those who believe in conspiracy theories that others dismiss as wacky nonsense. What makes conspiracy theories different from other beliefs is that the rules of truth are different. It is more than a sense of lowering the standards of evidence. Believing a conspiracy theory comes from thinking differently about reality leading to different beliefs about what is true. More on that later.

Three: Conspiracy theorists, because they believe truth claims that differ from common beliefs, think of themselves as different from "normal" people with a hint of superiority. Conspiracy theorists see themselves as having figured out secret *truths* that the rest of us have not. Believers in a conspiracy theory claim to have "knowledge" about seriously hidden, seriously dark skullduggery. Their "knowledge" sets them apart from the masses (that's you and me) who are "still duped" by the conspiracy.

The Three Dimensions of a Conspiracy Theory

Every conspiracy theory has those three components in varying degrees. There are also three dimensions to every conspiracy theory: paranoia, arrogance, and cliquishness.

The "they are out to get me" dimension

The long history of conspiracy theories is rooted in human paranoia about what lurks beyond what can be readily seen and heard. Concern about potential threats to our well-being is prudent. Obsessions with potential threats can be harmful. The "boogeyman" does not exist, except in the minds of those who fear him, and it is the fear itself that causes harm. Nevertheless, fear frequently outweighs sense and proportion, and the human imagination takes over. The "they are out to get me" dimension of conspiracy theories comes from paranoia taking over.

The boogeyman manifests itself in a wide range of conspiracy theories. Hatred and fear of people who are different is the primary cause of people believing in a conspiracy theory. Jews, Catholics, and Muslims have long been targets of suspicion and feature prominently as boogeymen in conspiracy theories.

The fraudulent document, "Protocols of the Elders of Zion,"[40] is a classic example of the "they are out to get me" conspiracy theory. The story of a secret cabal of Jews with a secret plot to overthrow the crown heads of Europe was

---

[40] Britannica, The Editors of Encyclopaedia, "Protocols of the Elders of Zion," *Encyclopedia Britannica*, May 29, 2024,
https://www.britannica.com/topic/Protocols-of-the-Elders-of-Zion.

concocted about 1903. It was an early version of what we now call "fake news." The Protocols conspiracy theory was, and still is, used by bigots to inflame hatred against Jewish people. It became a template for the common genre of conspiracy theories about shadowy people plotting to establish a world state.

Other fictitious world domination conspiracies are attributed to the Illuminati, the Freemasons, the Deep State, and similar groups, fictitious and real. There is little evidence that any of these conspiracies exist, but the conspiracy theorist can simply claim that the secret cabals are good at covering up evidence.

The "I know something you don't" dimension

Imagine I have a box. I tell you that I know that there is something incredible in the box, but I can't show it to you. You would laugh and walk away. The conspiracy theorist is not acting much differently. He knows something you don't, but he cannot show it to you because it is a secret. (I use "he" because conspiracy theorists are overwhelmingly male.)

Conspiracy theories are stories about what lurks beyond what can be readily seen and heard. On that blank canvas of the unknown, human imagination can flourish. Highly imaginative conspiracy theories spring up that tell us that something sinister is happening someplace we cannot see. The imaginative story can persist because it's about something that cannot be perceived; thus, the truth claims can't be verified, and the theory can't be easily refuted.

Such conspiracy theories include stories that there's a pedophile ring in a Washington, DC, pizza parlor[41]; that there are alien bases on the dark side of the moon or under the ice of Antarctica; that the Earth is hollow; that the Earth is flat; that the government has a secret space fleet; that the military

---

[41] Mike Wendling, "The Saga of 'Pizzagate': The Fake Story That Shows How Conspiracy Theories Spread," *BBC News*, 2 December 2016, https://www.bbc.com/news/blogs-trending-38156985.

has a crashed UFO at Area 51, and so on. You haven't been there, so you don't know otherwise. It's surprising there aren't conspiracy theories that the ocean is bottomless because most people have never been to the seafloor.

Anyway, beyond geography, any unknown or lesser known event leads to conspiracy theories sprouting from any ambiguity about what happened. For example, celebrity deaths spawn competing claims that the death was faked or caused by nefarious forces. The fact that some government activities are done out of the sight of the public inspires whispered allegations of nefarious intent. If there is a mystery, conspiracy theories about it will spring up to fill the gap in knowledge. A grim example of how imagination and opportunists fill in the unknown are the conspiracy theories that arose to explain the disappearance of flight MH370.[42]

The conspiracy theorist claims to have figured out a secret that "normal" people have not. This is the core element of any conspiracy theory. How it is that the conspiracy theorist knows these secrets is seldom adequately explained. Shadowy "insider sources" are cited, and when an alleged "insider" is quoted, his or her claims cannot be verified.

Always, it circles back to "it's a secret that I know, and you don't." Conspiracy theorists know what is in the box, but they cannot show you. You just have to believe them. You have to trust them. They are smarter than you, you know.

The "join the believers club" dimension
Cliques don't exist only in high school. If you believe in a conspiracy theory, you get to be part of a special club of fellow believers. This is largely human nature. People enjoy communing with others who share their interests. If you collect a thing—like coins or comic books—you can find others

---

[42] William Langewiesche, "Vanished: How Malaysia Airlines Flight 370 Disappeared." *The Atlantic*, June 17, 2019. https://medium.com/the-atlantic/vanished-how-malaysia-airlines-flight-370-disappeared-eccoafa78335.

who collect the same thing. If you collect rumors about a particular conspiracy theory, you can find others who do the same.

In a conspiracy theory community, you join more than a fan club. You join a distinct subculture. Depending on the nature of the conspiracy theory, members of the subculture of believers feel varying degrees of separation from mainstream society. Conspiracy theories centered on a story that "they are out to get us" can create subcultures that are insular and hostile to others. And if you don't believe their theory, well, you may be part of the conspiracy.

Conspiracy theorists can unite in a shared sense of accomplishment. The conspiracy theorists believe they "know" what is really going on while others remain in the dark. The conspiracy theory believers have joined an exclusive group of enlightened people who now have superior understanding that separates them from the "sheeple"[43] who are still in the dark, duped by the conspiracy. Believing a conspiracy theory can be more than agreeing with a belief—it can provide a sense of identity for people. More on that later.

Why Do People Believe in Conspiracy Theories?

We can start to see why conspiracy theories are attractive. We have seen three reasons already: paranoia about the unknown, feelings of accomplishment in knowing a secret, and connection with others who believe the conspiracy theory.

There are more reasons people choose to believe in conspiracy theories, the two main ones being a search for meaning and a search for profit. We see these two reasons in the two kinds of conspiracy theorists who have different objectives: earnest meaning seekers and con artists.

---

[43] Yes, it's a word. *Merriam-Webster.com Dictionary*, s.v. "sheeple," accessed June 19, 2024, https://www.merriam-webster.com/dictionary/sheeple.

Earnest meaning seekers

Granted, normal *is* boring, but some people turn to fantasy to spice things up. Many conspiracy theories are little more than fantasies. The world is an amazing and fascinating place, but some people feel the need for more. Those Egyptian and Mayan pyramids are amazing. Some people want to believe they are even more amazing—they were built by aliens. Similarly, some want to believe that Elvis didn't die, that he faked his death and lived on in secret. Princess Diana's death wasn't an accident; it was murder. COVID-19 wasn't just a horrific pandemic, it was a diabolical genetically engineered conspiracy.[44] And so on. Believing these stories makes the world seem more interesting.

Why the fantasies? Simply a need some people feel to manufacture a sense of self-worth. Believing in a conspiracy theory gives one a feeling that one is special because one has cracked the mystery of a secret conspiracy. "*I* figured that out, I am smarter than them." Then, the believer can manufacture the further belief that "they are out to get me" because of their knowledge of the conspiracy. "The government is spying on *me*," says the conspiracy theorist, "they are afraid of *me*," implying that he is important enough for shadowy cabals to spend time and effort on him. It gives some meaning to an otherwise bland and ordinary life.

Some conspiracy theory fantasies are harmless. Belief that the government is covering up bigfoot sightings probably isn't going to harm anyone. Other conspiracy theories that have political dimensions are less benign. People seek, in conspiracy fantasies, to replace their feelings of impotence and isolation with a more preferable and simplistic story that gives them a sense of certainty and meaning.[45]

---

[44] "Scientists Dispute a Suggestion that SARS-CoV-2 Was Engineered," *The Economist*, October 27, 2022, https://www.economist.com/science-and-technology/2022/10/27/scientists-dispute-a-suggestion-that-sars-cov-2-was-engineered.

[45] Mathew Hutson, "A Conspiracy of Loneliness," *Scientific American Mind*, Vol. 28 No. 3. May 2017, 15.

There are also prejudicial, ressentiment-fueled reasons for believing some conspiracy theories. For some, it is preferable to believe that Barack Obama was born in Kenya than that he is an American like them. For some, it is preferable to believe that 9/11 was an inside job than that the United States simply failed at defending itself. For some, it is preferable to believe that Russia interfered in an election than that their candidate simply lost. Being willing to hold such fantasies of sinister cabals inclines one to fall prey to con artists.

Con(spiracy) Artists

Earnest meaning seekers can be seduced by con artists. A con(spiracy) artist is a con artist whose con is being a professional conspiracy theorist. Through television and radio shows, Web sites, books, and lectures, they sell conspiracy theories as products. They have figured out a secret that "normal" people have not. They know what is in the box. They are smarter than all of the experts. You can hear about it if you buy the book, buy a subscription to the podcast, and so on.

The con(spiracy) artist sells an attractive fantasy. Well, attractive to a certain type of earnest person seeking a particular type of meaning that dumbs down the complexity of reality and replaces it with the false certainty that a conspiracy theory is true.

The granddaddy of today's breed of conspiracy theory con men is Erich von Däniken. His 1968 book, *Chariots of the Gods?*[46] was a bacchanalia of bad science and fallacious reasoning. It was an attack on expertise and academia, a sugar rush for earnest meaning seekers yearning to believe they are smarter than the experts and "normal" people. von Däniken's fantasy story that an alien civilization or civilizations intervened as gods in ancient human civilizations has

---

[46] Erich von Däniken, *Chariots of the Gods?* (Putnam, 1969–English version).

spawned a whole industry of con(spiracy) artists claiming to tell us what the experts are keeping secret.

Beginning in 1976, Zecharia Sitchin wrote a series of books in which he invented a fantasy of an extraterrestrial origin for humanity (aliens created us). He wisely chose to base his fantasy story on a group of minor Sumerian deities barely mentioned in ancient sources, so his fantasy was difficult to refute. It was a conspiracy theory in Sitchin's oft repeated accusation that "mainstream archaeology" was suppressing the truth.[47] Sitchin told people he knew what was in the box, even though no one else could see it. Perfect con.

Today, the ancient aliens con job is spearheaded by Giorgio Tsoukalos, who has great suits and great hair and a now 15-year-long television series, *Ancient Aliens*, peddling every wacky alien theory he can get his hands on. The show is slick and entertaining, mainly from the humor of its outlandish leaps of logic. For 252 episodes (and counting), *Ancient Aliens* has presented a parade of con(spiracy) artists pounding a constant drumbeat of "we have figured out secrets that the experts are suppressing."

I mention ancient aliens conspiracy theories in this book about people supporting Trump because these theories are gateways into more hardcore political conspiracy theories. Aliens and UFOs are a prolific con(spiracy) artist genre. Fantasies about aliens readily connect with conspiracy theories about sinister government forces and academia covering up all kinds of secrets. The *X-Files* TV show's stories of a deeply hidden government/alien conspiracy were fiction, but some people don't seem to have realized that.

The feeling of "we know more than the experts"—a feeling that resonates with ressentiment—easily transfers to any social and political issue. It is no coincidence that radio shows like *Coast to Coast AM* give platforms to con(spiracy) artists selling stories about aliens and the paranormal

---

[47] See especially: Zecharia Sitchin, *Genesis Revisited: Is Modern Science Catching Up with Ancient Knowledge?* (Avon Books, 1990).

alongside con(spiracy) artists selling various stories that "the government is out to get you." On right-wing radio, podcasts, and social media, you can hear stories about how the US secret space program has military bases all over the solar system, central banks are going to take all of your money, Atlantis is under Antarctica, Democrats are importing illegal immigrants to vote for them, gays are coming for your children, and the Illuminati have been poisoning the food supply with fluoride. (Fluoridation as a conspiracy is an old story. No, *Dr. Strangelove* didn't make it up.[48])

There is no shortage of con(spiracy) artists selling these and similar theories. The conspiracy theory industry creates a web of innuendo and skepticism for the earnest meaning seekers. In this environment of mistrust, political operatives can exploit an already primed audience.

Political Con(spiracy) Artists

Ancient alien con artists push the conspiracy theory that science suppresses archaeology. That is relatively harmless— just bilking people out of money. Far more malicious are the "government is out to get you" con(spiracy) artists. In this dark realm, the stories are nastier and powered by ressentiment-fueled value delusions, false moral judgments, and bigotry against particular groups of people. These conspiracy theories can inspire violence, such as storming capitol buildings. Political conspiracy theories come in varying virulence levels based on the subject of the theory.

Many people use conspiracy theories to express bigotry. The Nazis peddled the communist conspiracy and Jewish conspiracy theories to stoke violence and justify their dictatorship. Southern US white supremacists spread conspiracy theories about civil rights to keep minorities

---

[48] Catherine Carstairs, "Debating Water Fluoridation Before Dr. Strangelove," *American Journal of Public Health,* Aug;105(8), 2016, 1559-69.

suppressed. The Soviets and the United States both spread conspiracy theory propaganda during the Cold War to stoke xenophobia and justify militarism.

The "red menace" or "international communist conspiracy" has been a typical American political conspiracy theory. Such ideas were pushed by con(spiracy) artists such as Charles Coughlin, Joseph McCarthy, James Eastland, Lyndon LaRouche, and a plethora of right-wing radio talking heads, and these con men made political or commercial careers peddling theories of imminent anti-American conspiracies. "Communists are coming to steal your freedoms," was the constant refrain of the con(spiracy) artists.

After the Soviet Union fell, new boogeymen were needed and targeted. Today, gays, environmentalists, feminists, and basically everyone else more left wing than the con(spiracy) artist are branded as vile conspirators against "freedom" who are "out to get me, you, and your little dog, too." A recent incarnation of this political con job is QAnon: a fake person spewing fake news to stir up real hatred.[49]

Cultivating fear of the boogeyman has been a common political propaganda tool. Authoritarian governments, paramilitary groups, cult leaders, and others have used conspiracy theories to manipulate others. Shady operators have used the manipulative techniques of conspiracy theories to make money off of other people's fears.

For example, con(spiracy) artists leading the anti-vaccine movement sell falsehoods about the safety and effectiveness of vaccines. Their con game is that liberal governments and scientists "are out to get you" with vaccines.[50] The con(spiracy) artists tell people to ignore everything the government says. "Be afraid, despise the experts, send us

---

[49] Kevin Roose, "What Is QAnon, the Viral Pro-Trump Conspiracy Theory?" *New York Times*, Sep 3, 2021, https://www.nytimes.com/article/what-is-qanon.html.

[50] Richard M. Carpiano, et al, "Confronting the Evolution and Expansion of Anti-vaccine Activism in the USA in the COVID-19 Era," *Lancet*. 2023;401(10380):967-970.

money, and we will tell you how to protect yourself." Those con artists made money selling lies that have killed thousands worldwide.

Political conspiracy theories are effective at manipulation because they give believers a sense of identity. People can become part of a subculture of believers who define themselves as the opposition to the conspiracy. They can view themselves as brave people defending themselves from evil plotters. In some conspiracy theory subcultures, a near cultlike environment takes hold as described by people who escaped the QAnon conspiracy theory.[51]

Dedicated organizations like a political party or lobbying group can exploit the fear generated by conspiracy theories to strengthen loyalty to the group or cause. A party doesn't have to endorse a conspiracy theory explicitly to benefit from it; it only needs to be open-minded about it or slow to condemn it. We saw that strategy with the Republican Party, which was slow to condemn Trump's claims that the 2020 election was stolen. The earnest meaning seekers entered the space that the Republicans left open and now are perhaps more firmly pro-Republican than ever.

Conspiracy Theories in the Internet Age

Conspiracy theories are more common and widespread than ever. The Internet has catalyzed and concentrated conspiracy theories, providing forums for conspiracy theorists to gather and spread stories and fantasies. Anyone can post a conspiracy story or fantasy that potentially could be seen within minutes by hundreds or thousands all over the world.

The online world also strengthens conspiracy subcultures. Internet sites and forums create communication

---

[51] EJ Dickson, "Former QAnon Followers Explain What Drew Them In—And Got Them Out," *Rolling Stone*, September 23, 2020, https://www.rollingstone.com/culture/culture-features/ex-qanon-followers-cult-conspiracy-theory-pizzagate-1064076/.

silos or echo chambers lacking diverse voices. Followers of a conspiracy theory can speak with each other isolated from those who are "out to get us." Absolutist claims and conspiracy theories go not only unchallenged but receive only "likes" and "hell yeahs." By speeding the spread of propaganda and allowing users to feel a privileged sense in their consumption and sharing of information, the online world intensifies the three dimensions of conspiracy theories ("they are out to get us," "I know something you don't," and "join the believers club").

In the 2010s, YouTube became a hot spot for conspiracy theories. Side by side you could watch videos about bigfoot; UFOs; scientists hiding evidence of ancient civilizations; the world is flat; the world is hollow; JFK was killed by them, them, and the other people; world leaders are really lizard people; Obama is Kenyan, Russian, alien; the government is poisoning us, wants to imprison us, wants to take away guns, is trying to make us gay, is faking mass shootings, and is lying to us about anything and everything; oh, and Blacks/Jews/gays/ Muslims/commies/unions/feminists/immigrants are out to get us.

Alex Jones was king of the YouTube con(spiracy) artists, under his brand name, "InfoWars." He was perhaps the leading political con(spiracy) artist. Through videos and podcasts, Jones channeled the xenophobia of Charles Coughlin and updated it for the Internet age. Jones never met a right-wing conspiracy theory he wouldn't repeat and monetize.

Most notoriously, Jones unquestioningly repeated the fantasies of pizzagate and David Icke's reptilians, and he said the Sandy Hook massacre was a hoax. YouTube eventually removed con(spiracy) artist Alex Jones from its site, but Jones remained the vanguard for right-wing "they are out to get us" con(spiracy) artists online, making millions selling conspiracy porn to earnest meaning seekers.

Social media, despite its ability to connect with anyone anywhere, is predominantly used by people to commune only with those with whom they agree. Conspiracy theories are a rallying point for political activism. Because political activity today is more antagonistic toward others than supportive of one's own side, conspiracy theories are lubricant for political activism.

Creating conspiracy memes online is now an occupation for political groups. They are also political weapons. Before the 2016 election, both Hillary Clinton and Donald Trump promoters circulated stories that the other side would steal the election. That, after months of some Hillary supporters spreading bogus conspiracy theories that Bernie Sanders ran to sabotage Hillary's election.[52] They called Bernie supporters Russian trolls long before they called Trump supporters Russian trolls.

Trump and people who support him are even worse with their bigotry-driven conspiracy theories as the 2020 election cycle and its aftermath have shown. Using social media to spread conspiracy theories is now so integral to political campaigns that when Trump was no longer allowed to repeat on Twitter his Big Lie that the 2020 election was stolen, he invented his own social media platform. That platform is now a silo where people can listen to Trump and avoid differing opinions and fact-checking. Trump's Truth Social is one of the virtual worlds for conspiracy theorizing.

The World of the Conspiracy Theorist

Most of us take the world as it comes and, often to a fault, take things at face value. Conspiracy theorists perceive the world through a filter of suspicion. They take the world as

---

[52] Michael Sainato, "Bernie Sanders' Presidential Run Was Sabotaged by Fake News," *Observer*, November 30, 2016, https://observer.com/2016/11/bernie-sanders-presidential-run-was-sabotaged-by-fake-news/.

being full of deceit and malice. They may not believe the whole world is out to get them, but they believe a chunk of it is. If you are not with the conspiracy theorists, then they will assume you are against them. Because they assume you are against them, the conspiracy theorists are not interested in what you have to say. You are only trying to deceive them. The conspiracy theorists are always correct, and you and your evidence are always wrong. We are all "enemy" to them.

Many are amazed at how tightly conspiracy theorists cling to their theories, despite all evidence to the contrary. This is because their belief in the conspiracy theory is more than a truth claim—it is an identity claim. Members of a conspiracy theory subculture define themselves in terms of opposition to the conspiracy. That sometimes means opposition to just about everyone and everything. Hence, the need for tinfoil hats, metaphorical if not real, to keep everyone and the real world at bay. That kind of hatred is a very strong social glue, and it factors into conspiracy theory subcultures.

What ultimately lies behind conspiracy theories is ressentiment and the desire to get back at those who are different. Believing a conspiracy theory gives one feelings of meaning, power, and belonging. These feelings are normal and healthy. It is also normal and healthy to be wary of external threats to our well-being. The most effective way for con artists to manipulate people is to exploit normal and healthy human tendencies. When fear outweighs sense and proportion, often caused by manipulation, belief in conspiracy theories takes hold.

7. The Fine Line Between Patriotism and Jingoism

One day when I was a university undergrad, I was with a group of fellow students discussing a recent outbreak of armed conflict somewhere in the world. Being curious students, we talked about why the conflict had started.

"Because the ____ are proud to be ____," one person said (no need to prejudice the point by naming the conflict). Another person blurted out, "Why would they be proud to be ____?" I and others rebuked the person saying, "Why wouldn't they?"

It turned out that the young and naïve person sincerely believed that everyone in the world wished to be American rather than what they were. The idea that someone would fight to preserve a national or ethnic identity other than American was unthinkable to this person.

Then and now, what I find unthinkable is that person's attitude. There are two aspects to such an attitude. The first is that of course it is not only possible but also laudable for people to be proud of where they are from. The second is that the idea that everyone else wants to be like you is silly arrogance. These two aspects illustrate the fine line yet significant differences between patriotism and jingoism.

Pride in What?

Merriam-Webster defines "patriotism" as "love for or devotion to one's country."[53] I liken this human emotion of patriotism to one's love for and devotion to family. We naturally develop an attachment to where we came from. We also naturally gravitate toward the familiar.

---

[53] Merriam-Webster.com Dictionary, s.v. "patriotism," accessed June 20, 2024, https://www.merriam-webster.com/dictionary/patriotism.

This sense of patriotism is a good and noble sentiment. We should feel pride in our home and be willing to support and defend it. A society that is not supported by its members cannot survive. Patriotism is at its best when it is a communal spirit of neighbors helping neighbors.

However, pride is a double-edged sword—easily a virtue or a vice. Ressentiment, lazy thinking, and conspiracy theories can turn healthy pride into something nasty. When pride turns to hubris and hostility, patriotism morphs into jingoism. Merriam-Webster defines "jingoism"[54] as "extreme chauvinism[55] or nationalism marked especially by a belligerent foreign policy." I liken this human emotion of jingoism to bigotry. Really, that's what it is—bigotry toward others.

Unlike patriotism's noble sentiments of loyalty and building community, jingoism is an ugly sentiment of xenophobia. This is the case, despite the claims of the jingoists that they are patriots who are proud of their country.

Authoritarians call for "patriotism," and their political rhetoric centers on defense of the country. Again, loving and supporting one's home country is a positive sentiment. Is that what authoritarians and other right-wing self-proclaimed patriots are actually doing—simply loving and supporting their country? Is the distinction between patriotism and jingoism something substantial? Or is it a mere difference in terminology? What is going on in patriotism and jingoism?

Here's a way to think about it. Consciousness always takes an intention. If you are thinking of a tree, then the tree is the object of your conscious intention. Intention always occurs within an orientation—a set of beliefs and assumptions about the world and one's place in it.[56] The core difference between a

---

[54] Merriam-Webster.com Dictionary, s.v. "jingoism," accessed June 20, 2024, https://www.merriam-webster.com/dictionary/jingoism.

[55] Merriam-Webster.com Dictionary, s.v. "chauvinism," accessed June 20, 2024, https://www.merriam-webster.com/dictionary/chauvinism.

[56] Werner Stegmaier, *What is Orientation?* (DeGruyter, 2019).

patriot and a jingoist is the different orientations held by those two different people that lead them to different intentions.

A patriotic consciousness is oriented toward attachment and mutual recognition. It comes from an orientation of "we are in this together and need to help each other." Patriotism seeks peace and the building of one's own community.

A jingoistic consciousness is oriented toward detachment and misrecognition of those who are Other. It comes from an orientation of "we are superior to them, and we must defend ourselves from them." Jingoism may or may not actively seek conflict, but it is an orientation that assumes that conflict is inevitable and even laudable.

Both patriots and jingoists can legitimately claim to have attitudes of pride, but the intentions of their pride—in what they have pride—are different. Patriotism is pride in the tangible interpersonal connections among members of a community. Jingoism is pride in an idealized notion of what a country means, a mythic notion of its country as superior, a standard by which it can judge all other countries as inferior.

Honoring What Exactly?

We can see this distinction between patriotism and jingoism as something substantial in what each attitude honors. In the United States, for example, the professed purpose of Memorial Day is to honor those who died while serving their country. Many countries have a similar holiday commemorating their war dead. No doubt, there are many people who take that purpose to heart, honoring the individuals who were killed in war. I will dare to say that something else is at work beyond those instances of personal sincerity.

We are all taught to value someone for possessing positive traits. For example, we value people who are kind and giving to others. We are socialized into norms that direct which traits we should recognize and honor in others. But not all of the norms we are taught are fully benign—some are pathological, causing dis-ease. We are taught to honor those who died in wars, but what are we being socialized into recognizing and honoring?

There are two different social realities at work in the honoring of people who died in wars. One is the recognition of individuals—this intention is to remember and honor those people who served honorably. The other is the recognition of a power structure that exploits people in service of others' interests—this intention ignores those who suffered and died and instead is directed at the "glory" of war and the power of those who sent people off to die.[57]

War is a racket when it exploits and consumes people to make others richer and more powerful. Nationalistic jingoism is the propaganda tool used to convince and coerce people into being servants of wars in which they receive little if any benefit. Instead, many end up wounded or dead. Flowers on their graves won't help them.

That is not to suggest that there are never legitimate reasons to fight a war. The patriotic sentiment and communal spirit of neighbors helping neighbors lead people to recognize the value of the lives and well-being of compatriots and of defending those people from aggression.

Patriotism is a positive recognition norm. It values peace and mutual benefits. It is an orientation that builds communities and honors people.

Jingoism is a negative recognition norm. It values aggression and dominance. It is an orientation that destroys communities and people.

Jingoists claim to be patriots and use that claim to start wars. Many of the tyrants of history were jingoists. That's how pathological recognition works. It pretends to honor positive values and people, but it is a lie. Most wars are lies.

---

[57] Douglas Giles, *Rethinking Misrecognition and Struggles for Recognition* (Insert Philosophy, 2020), 106–107.

Back to the original story of that conversation years ago. Of course, people can be proud of their country, proud of where they are from, and will defend their homes and compatriots. But there is never a need to diminish someone else to feel good about yourself.

Again, patriotism is best when it is a communal spirit of neighbors helping neighbors because the conscious intention of patriotism is to help other people. That sometimes means being critical of the country's leaders and speaking out against injustice. That's another sharp distinction from jingoism, which demands that people not speak out against the authorities. Patriots only fight wars to defend the innocent. Jingoists start wars of aggression.

Which of America's wars were patriotic and which were jingoistic? I leave that for you to decide. Regardless, honor those who served, but do not glory in war.

8. Calvinism and the American Conception of Evil

Every country has its patriots and its jingoists. The United States is no exception to the general rule, but the jingoism of the United States has a distinct and exceptional character. Many people are familiar with the term "American exceptionalism." Trump and the people who support him definitely believe in the idea that America is distinct, and, of course, great. The idea of American superiority is the rhetorical and ideological centerpiece of the MAGA movement's jingoistic identity.

Stephen M. Walt defined American exceptionalism as "the idea that the United States is uniquely virtuous." He goes on to say that

> most statements of 'American exceptionalism' presume that America's values, political system, and history are unique and worthy of universal admiration. They also imply that the United States is both destined and entitled to play a distinct and positive role on the world stage. The only thing wrong with this self-congratulatory portrait of America's global role is that it is mostly a myth.[58]

The sentiment that the United States is a unique, morally superior country with a Manifest Destiny is a myth, but it is a very stubbornly persistent one. Why is that? Where did the idea come from and why has it stuck?

The jingoism of the American right wing has a particular character. Only the United States could create the vitriolic parochialism of the John Birch Society, the National Rifle Association, the Moral Majority, the Tea Party, QAnon, MAGA, and Trump. You may think that the hostile attitudes of

---

[58] Stephen M. Walt, "The Myth of American Exceptionalism," *Foreign Policy*, October 11, 2011, https://foreignpolicy.com/2011/10/11/the-myth-of-american-exceptionalism/.

these groups are sectarian throwbacks. You'd be correct. The reactionary worldview of today's American right wing, especially the reactionaries, has its roots in the Puritans of the 1600s and even before that in Switzerland in the 1500s.

What we see in the vitriol of American jingoists is a manifestation of the ideology of Calvinism. To understand America and its uniqueness, you need to understand John Calvin's unique political ideology and how Calvinism has shaped America.

Who Was John Calvin?

John Calvin was a political leader in Geneva, Switzerland, in the 1500s. He was a complicated person— vilified or exalted to unwarranted degrees; he has a legacy that is complex but undeniable.[59] He was never ordained as a pastor, but he invented his own version of Christianity, which he imposed on others. Politics and religion fit together hand in glove for Calvin, and this was one of his significant innovations.

Something Americans are not taught in school is that prior to Calvin, there was an understood rough separation between the Church and the secular state. No, the United States didn't invent but rather revived the idea. The medieval idea, deriving from the 400s with the Church Father Augustine, was that God chose separate leaders for church and state.

This is not to suggest that there wasn't significant meddling between nobility and clergy in each other's business, but the pretense of separate domains was always maintained. This was an important part of the feudal system. The Church supported and legitimized the king, and the king defended the

---

[59] A good biography of John Calvin is Alister E. McGrath, *A Life of John Calvin: A Study in the Shaping of Western Culture* (Wiley-Blackwell, 1993).

Church, but they were separate pillars that upheld the social structure.

Calvin saw the role of government as that of forcing citizens to declare loyalty to the correct doctrine. This wasn't a new idea among the fervently religious, but Calvin had little interest in respecting a separate domain for secular rulers, even if they pledged to defend the faith. He gave lip service to separation between church and state, but his doctrine and actions clearly indicated that in his version of religion—the religious declaration he established—the government should serve the dictates of the religious ministers.

During Calvin's time in Geneva, he continually battled with other elected leaders of the Geneva town council over control of the city's ordinances and judiciary. Politically, Calvinism is the ideology that its particular interpretation of the Christian religion should pervade all aspects of government and society. All dissent, political or religious, was deemed a criminal act against the state. Calvin wasn't the world's only theocrat, but his particular ideology has had an oversized effect on the United States.

What Was Calvin's Religious Doctrine?

To help explain the American reactionary Right, I need to dive briefly into a discussion of Calvin's theology. Bear with me; its relevance to the question of why some people support Trump will make sense once we get through it.

Calvin's religion was Protestant in that it was a break from the Catholic Church, but it was independent from other Protestant movements.[60] Calvin picked up on a recurring thread in some Christian sects—the cosmic view of dualism. Calvin's cosmology was an extreme dualism of Good versus Evil—God versus Satan—with humans stuck in the middle of

---

[60] John Calvin, *Institutes of the Christian Religion*, trans. Henry Beveridge (Hendrickson Publishers, 2008).

this cosmic war. God wants to save humanity, but Satan wants to drag humans into sin and devour them. In Calvin's view, God has allowed this world to belong to Satan, at least until the "end time." The world itself and the things in it are evil, including worldly pleasures, and Satan has many tricks to deceive people. Calvin used his political power to ban such activities as dancing because he deemed them to be sinful.

Calvin taught the doctrine of total depravity—that humans were fundamentally depraved and incapable of being good or of even knowing what is good. Only God is good, and only by God's direct action could a human think or act with moral goodness. The notion of total depravity was so central to Calvin's theology that it became known as the first point of the five points of Calvinism.[61]

People are so dominated by evil, Calvin taught, they are driven to sin. Since the original sin of Adam and Eve, people live in a world dominated by corruption and evil and are left in the clutches of Satan, the god of this age, who uses people for his own evil purposes. Calvin's worldview is that we are living in Satan's world, and the devil prowls outside your door.

Calvin believed that humans lacked free will because he believed that that reality was contrary to his conceptions of God's infinite power. He taught that in the world corrupted by original sin, God has given the world over to Satan. Humans' total depravity means they necessarily will to sin. In the sinful world, humans are in bondage to either God or Satan. Humans can't even choose who to serve. God preordained only some people to receive salvation (the "Elect"), leaving the rest of humanity to their depraved sinful nature and damnation to hell.

Like others who preach determinism, Calvin was not consistent in holding the view. He frequently fell back to

---

[61] R.C. Sproul, "TULIP and Reformed Theology: Total Depravity," *Ligonier Ministries*, March 25, 2017, https://www.ligonier.org/learn/articles/tulip-and-reformed-theology-total-depravity.

acknowledging individual free will tacitly, including for himself, but especially in teaching that others need to change their behaviors willingly to conform to Calvin's teaching.

Calvin's inconsistent view on determinism was that our salvation or damnation was determined by God but that we must still choose to resist Satan and sin and refuse to associate with sinful people. However, because people are depraved and the world is corrupted by sin, even the Elect can avoid sin only through God's intervention. Calvin further held that God intervened only to help the Elect, God granting them grace to resist sin, if they accepted it—a grace that Calvin said was irresistible.

One big problem Calvin had to deal with was that we are incapable of knowing the mind or choices of God. That would suggest that we can't know who God has determined are the Elect and who God has determined are the damned. (Never mind why God would choose such an arrangement—a question Calvin didn't seem to have considered.) This created a potential problem for the authoritarian state that Calvin believed needed to separate among the populace the sheep (the Elect) from the goats (those not Elect and in bondage to Satan), as the Bible says God will do on judgment Day.

Calvin's solution, consistent with the rest of his theology, was that God's grace has filled the Elect and compels them irresistibly toward good acts that yield good fruits. God will intervene for and bless the Elect but will not for those outside the Elect, the latter living mired in sin. Despite condemning worldly pleasures, Calvin taught that God gave worldly wealth and prosperity to the Elect and denied it to others.

This doctrine translated to two beliefs among the followers of Calvinism—that wealth is a sign of virtue and that poverty is conjoined with the corruption of moral depravity. Scholars have observed that these two beliefs that are embedded in Calvinism facilitated and justified the development of capitalism.[62]

The Polity of the Elect

Calvin, naturally, believed he was one of God's Elect and thus believed he was fit to rule as a sovereign. He was never officially the ruler over the city-state of Geneva, Switzerland, anymore than he was ever officially clergy. Calvin nevertheless wielded considerable political power and sought to establish a utopia (if you could call it that) of complete obedience to the rule of God's Law as interpreted by him and administered by his church. He developed the reputation as the "Tyrant of Geneva" because of his tactics in maintaining control over people's lives, including pushing for the execution of Michael Servetus.[63]

Calvin's new religion was popular in some circles in the 1500s and 1600s, although these groups lacked the political power to establish Calvinist-style autocracies. They were often brutally oppressed by rulers throughout Europe who saw these movements as a threat. Many Calvinists came to the New World hoping to establish their version of society there. The "Puritans" who came on the Mayflower to found New England were Calvinists who were seeking religious freedom of a sort.

Although most of America's "Founding Fathers" a century later were liberal in their Christianity, the Puritan influence on America has been profound. Good resources for studying this topic are *The Puritan Origins of the American Self*[64] and *The Puritan Origins of American Patriotism*.[65]

---

[62] Peter Feuerherd, "John Calvin: The Religious Reformer Who Influenced Capitalism," *JSTOR Daily*, July 10, 2017, https://daily.jstor.org/john-calvin-religious-reformer-influenced-capitalism/.

[63] Britannica, The Editors of Encyclopaedia. "Michael Servetus." *Encyclopedia Britannica*, April 8, 2024. https://www.britannica.com/biography/Michael-Servetus.

[64] Sacvan Bercovitch, *The Puritan Origins of the American Self* (Yale University Press, 1975).

[65] George McKenna, *The Puritan Origins of American Patriotism* (Yale

The United States is a nation that has always had a fierce strain of Calvinism that is still manifest today. The legacy of Calvin's version of religion created what Harold Bloom has called "the primary God of the United States."[66] This is the God of American exceptionalism, the Calvinist God who protects the United States, God's ordained world leader, from its enemies foreign and domestic. Citizens of the United States are God's Elect—at least those Americans who are good Calvinist Fundamentalists.

American Calvinism demands that others willingly change their behaviors to conform to Calvin's teaching about who is good and who is evil. That teaching includes the ideas that wealth is a sign of virtue and that poverty is conjoined with moral depravity.

The Worldly Consequences of Calvinism in the United States

Although few US denominations and churches will explicitly call themselves "Calvinist," the influence of Calvinism is strong among mainline and evangelical organizations. Organizational labels of "congregational," "reformed," "reconstructionist," and "fundamentalist" signify a connection with Calvinist doctrines. The American religious Right is fundamentally Calvinist in its view of the world.

Ethics is your response to how you believe the world is. The worldview of Calvinism is that humanity is divided between the sheep (the Elect) and the goats (those not Elect), and the world is corrupt, with Christians at war with satanic forces. Even if we are one of the Elect, we must remain on guard against Satan and his works. Calvin's determinism has been largely discarded given the need to convince people to

---

University Press, 2009).
[66] Harold Bloom, *Jesus and Yahweh: The Names Divine* (Riverhead, 2005), 111.

choose a godly life, which includes fighting against the ungodly.

Calvinist ethics responds to these beliefs with an ethical system that assumes that people are either inherently blessed by God or inherently corrupted by sin. This logically follows from the beliefs in predestination (God chooses who will be good or evil) and in God condemning sinners in absolute terms. Hell is a deserved eternal punishment, and the sentence is carried out without appeal, without hope of repentance or redemption.

Calvinist ethics therefore demands that good people, the Elect, condemn sinners, as they believe God condemns sinners, and shun them as enemies of the good. Calvin's strict dualism creates a gulf between those who are good and those who are evil. Even if that gulf could be bridgeable, it may not be worth the effort because evil people are totally depraved and probably irredeemably corrupted. They are wholly Other, and the good people must segregate themselves from the bad people.

Self-segregation is a common social tendency,[67] but Calvinism has a special version. Calvinist ethics demands not just that people are segregated but that good people be foot soldiers in the war against satanic forces. American Calvinists aren't just "Christians," they are *"Christian Warriors!"* To triumph over Satan requires

Logo of a Calvinist podcast

triumphing over people who believe differently from the Calvinist worldview. This fight is less against injustices or for

---

[67] Thomas A. DiPrete, et al. "Segregation in Social Networks Based on Acquaintanceship and Trust," *American Journal of Sociology* Vol. 116, No. 4 (January 2011), 1234-83.

expanding human rights and is more a right-wing effort to dictate others' beliefs and practices and to deprive others of rights and freedoms.

For example, in 2023, the United States saw a record number of attempts by right-wingers to ban books, 47% of the attempts targeting books by or about people who are nonheteronormative or of a racial minority.[68] These are attempts at censorship. These book bans are demanded not by Nazis, not by Soviets, but by organizations that justify their efforts with Calvinist-flavored ideals of the war against corruption and evil. The organizations claim to be protecting people (allegedly children) from content that is too explicit or offensive, but the constant thread of the book ban demands is the suppression of beliefs and practices contrary to Calvinist-inspired ideology and the homogenization of literature and ideas.[69]

This dynamic has been dramatized in such fictional works as *The Scarlet Letter*[70] and *The Crucible*.[71] In real life, this dynamic is repeatedly played out in American right-wing politics today, which sees the world in dualistic terms of "good" manifesting dominion over "evil" domestically and abroad. Calvinism gives American exceptionalism its sharp edge, turning it into a tool against a perceived corruption of purity and the reassertion of the traditional order.

If one holds the Calvinist worldview, the logical ethical response to the world is a two-tiered society in which power should be concentrated in the deserving people, with the undeserving people being deprived of power. Calvinism is certainly not the only worldview that gives impetus to a two-

---

[68] America Library Association, "Book Ban Data: Banned and Challenged Books," accessed June 22, 2024, https://www.ala.org/bbooks/book-ban-data.

[69] "Banned Books: Reasons Books are Challenged," *Butler University Information Commons*, accessed June 22, 2024, https://libguides.butler.edu/bannedbooks?p=217686.

[70] Nathaniel Hawthorne, *The Scarlet Letter* (Penguin, 2015).

[71] Arthur Miller, *The Crucible: A Play in Four Acts* (Penguin, 2003).

tiered society, but Calvinism has had an oversized influence on America's construction of its two-tiered society.

Secular Calvinism in the United States

Calvinist dualism provides the justification for America's two-tiered society of haves and have-nots. America's dualism is a manifestation of Calvinism's dualism. We see this in Christian Fundamentalism, where Calvinist doctrines have been the core dogma of the "religious right" for centuries, but by extension, this dualism is embedded in America's culture and power structure.

(Source: author)

Part of the legacy of Calvinism is its dualistic orientation in which those of different ethnicities or creeds are placed under the category of evil. Those considered different are vilified and marginalized. Foreigners are the enemy, especially if they are not white. People who aren't white, even though they are Americans, are considered lesser members of society. That Black people are cursed by God has been a long-held conception,[72] including by the American-born Church of Jesus Christ and Latter-day Saints.[73]

This Calvinist dualistic orientation has spilled over into secular America. A corollary to this conception of Good versus Evil is that attempts to help the disadvantaged in society are

---

[72] David M. Goldenberg, *The Curse of Ham: Race and Slavery in Early Judaism, Christianity, and Islam* (Princeton University Press, 2003).

[73] W. Paul Reeve, *Religion of a Different Color: Race and the Mormon Struggle for Whiteness* (Oxford University Press, 2015).

not only a waste of time but morally wrong. In essence, these attempts are aiding evil. The poor are poor because they deserve to be poor because they are sinful. The Calvinist worldview also lies at the root of the political ideology of libertarianism. Like Calvinism, libertarianism believes that a person's wealth and poverty reflect their ethical character rather than social realities. Throughout the right wing in America is the assumption that if someone is facing serious problems in their life, they probably did something to deserve it. We certainly shouldn't blame the injustices of the United States' two-tiered system.

The ideology and actions of people in the US right wing express Calvinist dualisms. The "Puritans" have always had an influence on American politics and culture that exceeds their numbers. The secular United States now has a civil religion built on the foundation of Calvinism.[74] The conservative notions of American exceptionalism, from the Monroe Doctrine and Manifest Destiny to its self-proclaimed status as "leader of the free world," are inspired by Calvinism.

The right wing's disdain for people who are different is an ethical view stemming from the belief that difference itself is a sign of moral failing. The Right's hostility to government helping the disadvantaged manifests the Calvinist belief that we should not help the undeserving. Reactionism on right-wing radio, television, and the Internet is the 21st century manifestation of the 16th century ideology of Calvinism.

Perhaps the most visible manifestation of secular Calvinism throughout US history has been anti-immigrant bigotry. We turn next to this distinctly American blend of ressentiment, conspiracy theories, and jingoism.

---

[74] Robert Neelly Bellah, "Civil Religion in America," *Journal of the American Academy of Arts and Sciences* 96 (1), 1967, 1–21.

9. America's Long History of Anti-Immigrant Rhetoric

CLOSE THE GATE.

—Orr in the Chicago *Tribune*.

1921 cartoon depicting immigrants as terrorists (fair use of public domain image)

Sometimes, listening to politicians such as Trump, one gets the impression that hordes of barbarians are massing at the borders. These politicians tell us to be very concerned about the threat of immigrants. What these barbarians are accused of isn't exactly clear; the message is vague beyond that good people should be afraid. These reactionary politicians and their surrogates make it seem that hostility against immigrants is fiercer than ever. History records otherwise.

Many people feel a need for separation from those different from them,[75] especially when that separation has an air of superiority to the others. Immigrants can easily be cast in that role of separate inferiors, though many people who look down on immigrants prefer those immigrants remain in their countries of origin.[76]

That need for separation pervades anti-immigrant sentiments throughout Europe, the United States, and Canada. Separateness has long been a justification for national pride, however false and perverse. The British can be slightly (only slightly) forgiven because the slender channel of water between England and the rest of Europe has given the British a sense of separateness. The rest of Europe still suffers from the "fear of the Turk" mentality,[77] but it has been centuries since that threat was real. Cultural habits sometimes fade away slowly.

I previously stated that Trump doesn't really say anything new. That is especially true of his attacks on and scare tactics about immigrants to the United States. Ressentiment about the presence of immigrants—people who are different—has a long history in the United States.

The history of American anti-immigrant bigotry is a history of its immigration patterns. What we see in the MAGA movement—the reactionism, the ressentiment, the lazy thinking leading to bigoted conspiracy theories, the jingoism, the Calvinist dualism, and "America First" attitude—we can see repeatedly in past anti-immigrant movements. This is part of that particular strain of political culture that I mentioned at the beginning of the book. It is a strain unique to the United

---

[75] DiPrete, et al. "Segregation."

[76] Tyler Anbinder, "The Long, Ugly History Of Insisting Minority Groups Can't Criticize America," *The Washington Post*, July 19, 2019, https://www.washingtonpost.com/outlook/2019/07/19/long-ugly-history-insisting-minority-groups-cant-criticize-america/.

[77] Carina L. Johnson, "Mobilizing Fear: Propagandizing German–Ottoman Conflict," *The American Academy in Berlin*, accessed June 26, 2024, https://www.americanacademy.de/mobilizing-fear/.

States deriving from the country's unique history. This mixture of cultural attitudes currently takes Trump as its center of focus, but Trump is simply its most recent focus.

American Exceptionalism Again

Some might suggest that the Atlantic Ocean gave people in the United States a sense of separation that explains some of the resistance to immigration. The problem is that, except for the long-suppressed indigenous populations of the Americas, everyone living in the United States is a descendant of immigrants. And yet, every generation of Americans has seemed intent on slamming the door on new immigrants despite each generation being in the United States because they or their immediate ancestors were immigrants. That idea was captured brilliantly by this cartoon that appeared in *Puck Magazine* on January 11, 1893.

J. Keppler's 1893 cartoon (fair use of public domain image)

Close the gates, raise the drawbridge, keep out the undesirable newcomers. A nation of immigrants against immigrants.

America has been filled with generation after generation of people who wanted to be the new elites and keep out the "riffraff" of the next generation of immigrants. Such feelings of ressentiment toward newcomers stem from a desire many people have to conserve the perceived purity of the traditional order. This is the purity to which Jason Stanley referred as right-wing politicians' real meaning of the term "corruption."[78]

In the case of America's anti-immigrant ressentiment, the fear that immigrants will corrupt America reflects the paradoxical myth of American exceptionalism. America suffers from the "city on a hill syndrome," described by Andrew Kohut and Bruce Stokes as "Americans' belief that America is a shining city on a hill—a place apart where a better way of life exists to which all other peoples should aspire."[79] The paradox is the belief that America is so exceptional that everyone should want to come here, but if they do, it will corrupt America.

---

[78] Stanley, *How Fascism Works,* 36.
[79] Andrew Kohut and Bruce Stokes, "The Problem of American Exceptionalism," *Pew Research Center*, May 9, 2006, https://www.pewresearch.org/politics/2006/05/09/the-problem-of-american-exceptionalism/.

"Riff Raff" cartoon by Louis Dalrymple, 1903
(fair use of public domain image)

By 1903, the hyperbolic depiction of immigrants as subhuman vermin infecting American shores was commonplace. These vicious characterizations were reactionary responses to the increasing cultural diversity of the immigrant populations that had been arriving since the 1870s. "Close the gates" and "shut the doors" weren't just sentiments from 1921, 1903, 1893 or 1903, much less Trump's claim in 2023 that immigrants were "poisoning the blood of our country."[80] Those demands to exclude new immigrants have always been woven into the fabric of the United States, even though the cloth was made of immigrants.

---

[80] Marianne LeVine and Meryl Kornfield, "Trump's Anti-immigrant Onslaught Sparks Fresh Alarm Heading into 2024," *The Washington Post*, October 12, 2023, https://www.washingtonpost.com/elections/2023/10/12/trump-immigrants-comments-criticism/.

We can go back even further in US history. The first anti-immigrant laws were the Alien and Sedition Acts of 1798.[81] In addition to establishing "alien" as the definition of immigrants, these laws gave the government broad powers to deport immigrants deemed "dangerous" and to ban speech and publications deemed "false, scandalous, and malicious." These laws were passed only seven years after the First Amendment was ratified that forbade the government from "abridging the freedom of speech, or of the press." The double standard of American ideals and laws not applying to new immigrants, indigenous, and enslaved people began in the country's infancy.

Slamming the Door on the Germans and the Irish

European immigration to the United States started to escalate significantly around 1840, when millions of Irish and German Catholic people began arriving. Largely because of Calvinist anti-Catholic bigotry, there was significant resistance to these immigrants.

A direct predecessor to the MAGA movement in ideology and practices arose in 1844. Lewis Charles Levin founded a new political party to fight what he alleged was a Catholic conspiracy to take over the United States. They first called themselves the "Native American Party" (apparently unaware of the irony), eventually shortened to the "American Party," and eventually they became the Know-Nothing Party (more irony). This political party invented the term "nativist," a term still used to describe anti-immigrant political parties worldwide.[82]

---

[81] "Alien and Sedition Acts (1798)," *The U.S. National Archives and Records Administration*, accessed June 21, 2024, https://www.archives.gov/milestone-documents/alien-and-sedition-acts.
[82] Lorraine Boissoneault, "How the 19th-Century Know Nothing Party Reshaped

Xenophobic and bigoted, the party spread disinformation and conspiracy theories about immigrants and Catholics; established a secret fraternal society; and sponsored paramilitary gangs that harassed and terrorized perceived enemies, including burning down Catholic churches. In many respects, the American Know-Nothing Party had all the attributes we would now say are indicative of a reactionary movement like MAGA.

When the potato blight of 1846 to 1852 devastated crops in Europe, especially in Ireland, desperate immigrants came to the United States. They were met with an established anti-Catholic movement that attempted to demonize the Irish people. From the 1840s to the 1890s, Irish people were subjected to violence and abuse and were libeled as drunks and violent ingrates.

In the 1860s, the language in job postings of, "No Irish need apply," was so common it inspired a popular song with that title.[83] Despite widespread hostility, Irish immigrants thrived in many areas, eventually becoming part of the establishment in cities like Boston and Chicago.

A sharp increase in German immigration to the United States occurred in the 1860s and 1870s. A large number of people from what is now southern Germany immigrated in response to the unification of most German-speaking lands under Prussian dominance. Germans soon became the largest immigrant population in the United States. Their large number (by 1890, there were an estimated two million German Catholics in the United States)[84] and the reality that they were mostly Catholic sparked anti-German hostility.

American Politics," *Smithsonian Magazine*, January 26, 2017, https://www.smithsonianmag.com/history/immigrants-conspiracies-and-secret-society-launched-american-nativism-180961915/.

[83] Poster of the lyrics of the song available from Everett, "Anti-Irish Song. No Irish Need Apply," *FineArtAmerica*, accessed June 29, 2024, https://fineartamerica.com/featured/anti-irish-song-no-irish-need-apply-everett.html?product=poster. No endorsement implied.

[84] American Catholic History Research Center and University Archives, "German

The prohibition movement of the time (partially inspired by Calvinism) attempted to capitalize on anti-German sentiments by targeting the German practice of consuming alcohol on Sundays. Oh, the horrors. As too often is the case, people with different customs unnerved other people who lacked an open mind and developed ressentiment against the newcomers. The earlier generations of immigrants wanted to shut the door behind them. The newcomers with their own customs were corrupting the purity of Calvinist tradition.

Slamming the Door on the Chinese

In the 1860s, many immigrant laborers from China helped built the American West—in particular, the railroads. Other laborers of other ethnic heritages, mostly immigrants, also contributed, but the Chinese were singled out for hostility. This was likely because Chinese immigrants were even more foreign to the Anglo-American Calvinist ideal than were the Irish and German immigrants.

Chinese immigrants were refugees fleeing wars in China in the 1850s and early 1860s.[85] They were hired en masse by the railroad corporations to work on the transcontinental railroad completed in 1869. Many Chinese immigrants settled in the new West Coast states, especially California.

Later, as massive numbers of Americans migrated from the Eastern States to California, they clashed with the already established Chinese people. As is so often the case in anti-immigrant bigotries, the Americans, though they were the newcomers to the region, insisted that the Chinese people "did not belong" there. In Los Angeles in 1871, a mob attacked the

---

Immigrants," *The Catholic University of America*, accessed June 21, 2024, https://cuexhibits.wrlc.org/exhibits/show/turning-toward-a-new-century--/a-diverse-church/german-immigrants.

[85] "Chinese Migrations in the Mid-Late 19th Century," *Asia Pacific Curriculum*, accessed June 21, 2024, https://asiapacificcurriculum.ca/learning-module/chinese-migrations-mid-late-19th-century.

Chinese neighborhood, killing at least 19 Chinese people.[86] Similar to the racist attacks on Black Americans in the Deep South, riots, pogroms, and legalized racial segregation and exclusion were inflicted on people of Chinese heritage across Western States.

Local, state, and even federal laws were enacted denying equal rights to Chinese people. The Naturalization Act of 1870 granted citizenship to former slaves of African descent but specifically denied any possibility of US citizenship to Chinese immigrants. That act was part of a series of laws passed that targeted Chinese people for discrimination, culminating in the Chinese Exclusion Act of 1882 that banned most Chinese people from entry into the United States.[87] It remains the only law in US history that specifically banned people from a particular nation. The earlier generations of immigrants wanted to shut the door behind them.

Slamming the Door on Southern and Eastern Europeans

Another massive increase in immigration to the United States began in the 1870s. New in this wave was the increase in people coming from Italy and Eastern Europe. This change gradually shifted the focus of anti-immigrant ire away from the Irish and Germans, who by the time of the Immigration Act of 1924 had become the more desirable, or less undesirable, immigrants. The Immigration Act of 1924 set entry quotas for all other nations, but the primary impetus for

---

[86] Shelby Grad, "The Racist Massacre that Killed 10% of L.A.'s Chinese Population and Brought Shame to the City," *Los Angeles Times*, March 18, 2021, https://www.latimes.com/california/story/2021-03-18/reflecting-los-angeles-chinatown-massacre-after-atlanta-shootings.

[87] Marian L. Smith, "Race, Nationality, and Reality: INS Administration of Racial Provisions in U.S. Immigration and Nationality Law Since 1898," *Prologue Magazine,* Vol 34, No. 2, 2002, https://www.archives.gov/publications/prologue/2002/summer/immigration-law-1.

the quotas was to curtail immigration from Southern and Eastern Europe.[88]

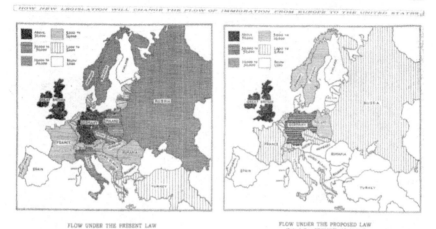

AMERICA OF THE MELTING POT COMES TO END

Effects of New Immigration Legislation Described by Senate Sponsor of Bill—Chief Aim, He States, Is to Preserve Racial Type as It Exists Here Today

FLOW UNDER THE PRESENT LAW   FLOW UNDER THE PROPOSED LAW

New York Times infographic from 1924 defending the Immigration Act of 1924. (fair use of public domain image)
"To preserve racial type as it exists here today"—a major driver of anti-immigrant attitudes then and now

Although not as fierce as it was against the Chinese, the prejudice against immigrants from Southern and Eastern Europe was strong. These people were demonized as subhuman vermin. Italian immigrants were stereotyped as violent degenerates, assassins, brigands, and mafiosi. Immigrants from Eastern Europe, Slavs and Jews, were stereotyped as diseased and impoverished vagrants.

That most immigrants did not have great wealth was not surprising. Those well-placed in Europe's class hierarchy had less reason to leave to seek better opportunities in the United States. The American Calvinist notion that poverty was a sign

---

[88] "The Immigration Act of 1924 (The Johnson-Reed Act)," *Office of the Historian, US State Department*, accessed June 30, 2024, https://history.state.gov/milestones/1921-1936/immigration-act.

of immorality enhanced the xenophobic bigotry against immigrants. Berating immigrants as vermin was commonplace—again, children of immigrants wanting to close the door behind them.

Detail of "Direct from the Slums of Europe" cartoon by Louis Dalrymple, 1903.
(fair use of public domain image)
The use of Uncle Sam imagery in Dalrymple's cartoons is a clear symbol of
American purity that needs to be defended from immigrants.

Slamming the Door on War Refugees

After the end of World War I, anti-immigrant anxiety took on the double fears of an ingress of people displaced by the war and of the specter of Bolsheviks. The displaced persons fell under the stereotype of impoverished vagrants. The now well-worn paths of discrimination and exclusion to preserve the purity of America applied to these new immigrants, leading to the previously mentioned entry quotas of the Immigration Act of 1924.

The Bolshevik question was a different matter, however. The overthrow of the czar in Russia unsettled many throughout the Western world, especially capitalists and business owners. The stereotype of immigrants as criminals blended easily with the new anxiety that immigrants from Eastern Europe would be similarly minded revolutionaries. How real the threat was to the United States has never been clear, but the fear was palpable.

The United States had seen violence from anarchists since the late 1880s, mostly small-scale riots, sabotage, and bombings. The most significant incident was when an anarchist, and child of Polish immigrants, assassinated President William McKinley in 1901.[89] The ironic hypocrisy was that riots, bombings, and killings of Blacks, Catholics, and Chinese people by nonanarchist whites were socially acceptable.

In 1919, a wave of coordinated anarchist bombings shook the United States, mainly perpetrated by a group of Italian immigrants who for the previous five years had engaged in a terrorist campaign of more scattered bombings.[90] They weren't Bolsheviks or Marxists, but in the political environment, it was easy to blame the "Reds." The first Red Scare began in 1919. It was a conspiracy theory and propaganda campaign that targeted leftists; labor unions; and, of course, immigrants. People, being lazy thinkers unwilling to distinguish differences, found it was easier to tar all of them with the same brush as corruptors of the American way. The "Close the Gate" cartoon at the beginning of this chapter smearing all immigrants as violent extremists, was typical of

---

[89] "William McKinley Assassination: Topics in Chronicling America," *Library of Congress*, accessed June 30, 2024, https://guides.loc.gov/chronicling-america-william-mckinley-assassination.

[90] Charles H. McCormick, *Hopeless Cases: The Hunt for the Red Scare Terrorist Bombers* (University Press of America, 2005).

this period. To be a foreigner was to be an enemy. The xenophobia of "they hate our liberty" entered the political conversation.

The Classist Component

There has long been a classist component to the United States' anti-immigrant sentiment. No one much minded the wealthy immigrant. The working-class immigrant was suspect because all working-class people were suspect. Again, the influence of Calvinism was present. It was an ancient prejudice that in America blended well with nativist bigotries. That new immigrants were "coming to steal our jobs" had some truth to it, but it was and still is a hypocrisy that the land of immigrants sought and still seeks to oppress and exclude new immigrants.

These latest anti-immigrant movements coincided with the rise of the concentrated power of the American industrialists and robber barons—the so-called Gilded Age.[91] The wealthy right wing in the United States exploited fears of immigrants to advance their own agendas to keep control over commodity trusts[92] and stoke fears against labor unions, which represented many immigrant laborers.[93] It was easy because the press they controlled (right-wing dominance of newspapers from 1870 to 1920 was far greater than in the media today) linked the growing labor union movement with undesirable immigrants, anarchists, and Bolsheviks; the political rhetoric we hear today is nothing new.

Anti-immigrant rhetoric has been a political weapon throughout US history. Right-wing politicians use anti-

---

[91] Sean Dennis Cashman, *America in the Gilded Age, Third Edition* (New York University Press, 1993).
[92] Charles R. Geisst, *Wall Street: A History* (Oxford University Press, 1999).
[93] Stanford University Press, "Capital and Labor" in *The American Yawp*, accessed June 22, 2024, http://www.americanyawp.com/text/16-capital-and-labor/.

immigrant rhetoric to distill reactionaries' feelings of xenophobic ressentiment. The formula has been to use scare tactics and conspiracy theories to connect with people who believe in the myth of American exceptionalism. It works. Many politicians and con(spiracy) artists have used the anti-immigrant strategy to gain power.

Today, right-wing politicians, all descendants of immigrants, are slamming the door on immigrants—in particular, Latin Americans, Muslims, and South Asians. This is the xenophobia with which we are most familiar today, but at its rotten roots lie the same bigotries that have long festered in the United States. The reactionary political power dynamic is the same today as it was in the 1840s and each decade since.

Trump is the current focal point for the most recent manifestation of this age-old thread of American culture. Whether he believes his anti-immigrant, anti-foreigner rhetoric is unimportant. A significant number of Americans have those xenophobic views, and they will support politicians they believe hate the same people whom they hate.

10. Let's Call Bigotry What It Is

When signs like these could be displayed openly, was this when America was "great?"

Signs from the country of genocide, slavery, and segregation
(fair use of public domain images)

Of course, the feelings expressed by such signs were not shared by all Americans, but we can't ignore the historical reality that these feelings have had a significant effect on the United States. Nor can we say these feelings can be summed up as racism. Of course, they are racist feelings, but our diagnosis can't end there. The hatred spewed within ignorant racist views is a symptom of a deeper dis-ease. We need to call racism what it really is—something that is larger than any individual but that is an emotion that springs from the individual weakness that is bigotry. First, let's deal with what bigotry really is.

Circling Back to the Strongest Power in Politics

As discussed earlier, ressentiment is exploited by politicians and con(spiracy) artists adept at distilling reactionaries' fear of diversity and their desire to reassert the traditional order of power hierarchies. That leaders can exploit fear to manipulate people into a social force doesn't negate the reality that it is weakness that is being manipulated and channeled.

The bitter irony of institutional racism is that it is weakness empowered. Racism is a perverse social structure that consolidates and empowers weak, fearful people. The power structure of racism says, "believe these stories, and you don't have to deal honestly with your fear." Structural racism says, "it's okay to be afraid of the evil Other, you don't need to treat them as equal human beings." Racism is a social structure that empowers unthinking fear.

Racism is a structure built on weakness. It is powerful because it is a power structure of social institutions that condone and even encourage individuals to be bigoted. In institutional racism, oppression of minorities is recognized as social norms that are embedded in our social existence, but the norms are based on value delusions about others.

Nietzsche was correct on that point—that feelings of ressentiment in its weakness create an enemy against which one contrasts oneself as the good.[94] Structural racism is a hierarchical power structure maintained by ressentiment, and

---

[94] Nietzsche, *Genealogy*.

its social norms give cover under which value delusions can hide. The social norms of racism are enforced by the legal system and spread far and wide by the media. Society teaches false views of minorities to individuals who receive social recognition when they repeat those lies.

The structural bigoty of all types in the United States is part of the country's secular Calvinism. Those considered different are vilified and marginalized. People who are not white, women (especially feminists), religious minorities, nonheteronormative people, and others, even though they are Americans, are considered lesser members of society. The Calvinist influence on secular legal and governmental structures is significant but is unquestionably even more influential in the American religious Right. As in other social areas previously discussed, there is a distinctly American strain of right-wing religion.

Fearful Reactions

Racism is a symptom. All forms of bigotry are symptoms. Even ressentiment, the feeling that is the core motivator of all forms of bigotry, is a symptom. Max Scheler is correct that ressentiment, and all the harm that feeling causes, takes its root in weaknesses from which the people harboring it suffer.

We all have a natural fear of the Other—anything that is different—but especially people who differ from us in their values and customs.[95] How we deal with that fear is the difference between maturity and immaturity. A person has bigoted thoughts and feelings because they've given in to that fear of the Other, and this weakness is the impotency to which Scheler was referring as ressentiment.

---

[95] F. Diane Barth, "How Can We Understand Our Fear of the Other?" *Psychology Today*, March 11, 2016, https://www.psychologytoday.com/us/blog/the-couch/201603/how-can-we-understand-our-fear-the-other.

It takes a certain degree of courage to accept people for who they are and how they are. It's easier to deal with and accept people who are similar to oneself. Differences cause tensions, and not everyone has the wherewithal to deal maturely with those tensions.

We certainly can't accept some differences. We don't accept men who feel it is okay to molest children. We don't accept people who cheat others, who steal from others, and so on. We need to maintain values that support other people, and that means passing judgment on those who harm others.

But to refuse to accept people because they drink beer on Sundays, dress differently, or speak a different language doesn't seem to transgress ethical values. And yet, these were the intolerances of difference behind some anti-immigrant feelings.

It is difficult to know where to draw the lines on accepting or passing ethical judgment against people's behaviors. It requires an ongoing practice of a great deal of personal reflection and rational contemplation. But people are lazy thinkers. It is easier to shirk one's responsibility and accept stereotypes and conspiracy theories about other people. It is easier to give into fear of the Other.

Bigoted actions, including racism, are fearful reactions to others. People feel hatred because they can't cope with difference. To cover up our fears and justify our fearful reactions, we make up stories about others. Actually, we usually don't need to. We can adapt the stories that were made up before us. We use the stories to convince ourselves that we're right to fear and hate others.

Our stories tell us that those who are different from us are inferior to us. They are immoral. Stupid. Deviant. Dangerous. We invent names to dehumanize them and brand them with these labels that become profanities and insults. Bigoted labels become weapons powered by ressentiment to harm others and deny them human rights. Labels unite individual fearful reactions into groups united by ressentiment. Scheler was correct that these feelings of ressentiment can permeate a whole culture or era and an entire moral system, as has been continually present in the United States and its institutional structures of racism.

The difference between personal bigotry and racism is the possession of power. Racism is rooted in bigotry, but the two are not the same. There is a difference between personal thoughts and feelings and macrosocial structures.

Anyone can have bigoted opinions because anyone can be ignorant and fearful. But not everyone has the social power to act on their bigoted opinions. To take two extreme examples: Bigotry against Jewish people was common throughout Europe for centuries, but it took the structural power of the Nazi regime to engineer the Holocaust. Also during World War II, but in the United States, bigotry against Japanese people was common, but it was the structural power of the US military that incarcerated Japanese-Americans in concentration camps.[96]

A present-day example is that police and politicians can believe that all Black people are inferior, *and* they have the social power to act on that belief. In contrast, an individual person can believe that other people are inferior but have no social power to act on that belief. Any individual can be bigoted, but it takes the power of social institutions to be racist. That's why institutions like segregation and apartheid can exist far more easily than can movements to oppose institutional racism.

---

[96] "Japanese-American Incarceration During World War II," *National Archives,* last reviewed on March 22, 2024, https://www.archives.gov/education/lessons/japanese-relocation.

11. "Christian" Nationalism

All of the preceding discussion in this book contributes to understanding why some people support Trump. Vested with that knowledge, we now turn to the particularly vexing paradox of why the religious Right supports Trump, and not only supports him but sees him as one of theirs and even as being a kind of God-sent savior to America.

There's little evidence that Trump has any religious beliefs or practices. It seems that the closest he has come to any sort of religious conviction is a familiarity with the guilt-free gospel of Norman Vincent Peale's program of positive thinking to attain wealth and success.[97]

Trump is most likely America's first atheist president. Even if he doesn't go that extreme in his beliefs, the idea that he is a man of faith, or any kind of serious Christian, is indeed preposterous.[98]

And yet, Trump is associated with and embraced by the religious Right. An October 2023 poll found that more than half of Republicans polled said Trump was a person of faith, ahead of every other candidate who had then announced for the Republican nomination, including even Mike Pence, who could not possibly be more open about his Calvinist faith. The other remarkable takeaway from the poll was that only 23% of Republicans said that Joe Biden was a man of faith, the Joe Biden who is very open about his Catholic faith. In contrast, the poll found only 14% of Democrats said Trump was a man of faith but 63% of Democrats said Biden was a man of faith. The numbers led the newspaper that commissioned the poll to

---

[97] Daniel Burke, "The Guilt-Free Gospel of Donald Trump," *CNN*, October 24, 2016, https://www.cnn.com/2016/10/21/politics/trump-religion-gospel/index.html. Chris Lehmann, "The Self-Help Guru Who Shaped Trump's Worldview," *In These Times*, December 13, 2017, https://inthesetimes.com/article/Trump-White-House-Self-Help-Norman-Vincent-Peale-MAGA.

[98] David Mills, "The Dangerous Christian Belief that Donald Trump Is a 'Man of Faith,'" *Pittsburgh Post-Gazette*, June 22, 2024, https://www.post-gazette.com/opinion/david-mills/2024/01/08/david-mills-evangelicalism-trump-christianity/stories/202401080097.

quite reasonably conclude that "the perception of Trump as a man of faith was more related to voters' political identity than their religious identity."[99]

The religious Right's embrace of Trump includes the embrace by people within the "Christian" nationalist movement. This movement claims that the United States was founded as a Christian nation and must be preserved as a Christian nation. This vision is intertwined with the belief that America is a shining city on a hill, a metaphor with biblical undertones from Jesus's Sermon on the Mount.[100]

With the other US political movements we've already discussed, "Christian" nationalism predates Trump's arrival on the political stage. The ethnoreligious nationalist patterns and logics of current "Christian" nationalism are the old ethnoreligious nationalist patterns and logics of Calvinist dualism and anti-immigrant movements. There is little new here.

Let's Call "Christian" Nationalism What It Is

This "Christian" nationalist movement is not Christian; it's reactionism, that particular strain of Calvinist American reactionism that helped birth the United States but has ever since kept it in a firm grip of ressentiment. It is more political than religious, and it is extreme right wing.

Jason A. Springs refers to the movement as "zombie nationalism."[101] Springs argues persuasively that the religious

[99] Suzanne Bates, "Poll: Republicans see Trump as a 'Person of Faith' ... More so than Mitt Romney, Mike Pence and Others," *Deseret News*, September 26, 2023, https://www.deseret.com/2023/9/26/23891360/trump-biden-man-of-faith-religious-mitt-romney-vivek-ramaswamy/.

[100] Jesus (attributed), "You are the light of the world. A city situated on a hill cannot be hidden," Gospel of Matthew 5:14, *King James Version*.

[101] Jason A. Springs, "Zombie Nationalism: The Sexual Politics of White Evangelical Christian Nihilism," In ed. Atalia Omer and Joshua Lupo, *Religion, Populism, and Modernity: Confronting White Christian Nationalism and Racism* (University of Notre Dame Press. 2023), 51-99.

nationalism—and white Christian nationalism in particular—that currently supports Trump is an expression of established elective affinities around white ethnicity, evangelical religion, gender, and sexual politics that recur in reaction to periods of rapid social change and diversification. Springs attributes zombie nationalism to feelings driven by racialized religious grievances symptomatic of Nietzsche's concept of ressentiment.

Scheler's concept of ressentiment is more salient and useful in understanding "Christian" nationalism as what Springs calls "zombie" nationalism. That's because in Nietzsche's conception, ressentiment is the contemptuous reaction of weak people to strong and noble people.[102] This is not compatible with the reactionism of "Christian" nationalism, which despises and seeks to further disempower the already marginalized—people who are not perceived as white, women, nonheteronormative people, and others. What Springs describes as the "exclusionary patterns of racism, ethnocentrism, heteronormativity, and patriarchy that fuel the engine of ressentiment animating zombie nationalism"[103] are better explained by Scheler's broader concept of ressentiment and how his conception explains social movements.

The politically reactionary and exclusionary nature of "Christian" nationalism is not Christian, not by any reasonable measure. It is American nationalism—distinctly American and thoroughly jingoistic. It is a form of identity politics, asserting that its version of American identity is morally superior and deserving of greater power in society and government. The movement is, as Katherine Stewart has dubbed it, power worshippers who are engaging in an organized quest for power.[104] As with all right-wing movements, this movement is a quest for greater concentration of power—their worship of

---

[102] Nietzsche 21-22.
[103] Springs, Zombie Nationalism," 51.
[104] Katherine Stewart, *The Power Worshippers: Inside the Dangerous Rise of Religious Nationalism* (Bloomsbury Publishing, 2022).

power turning them into unthinking zombies filled with ressentiment and jingoism susceptible to conspiracy theories and those who can manipulate their fears.

The power worshippers wrap their nationalism in a caricature of Jesus just as they wrap their bigotry in the American flag. They have locked Jesus and Christianity in a gilded cage of American nationalism, having fabricated and erected their own White Jesus--a distinctly American version of the Northern European White Jesus. American nationalism created its own religion—a distinctly American version of Calvinism that hijacked terms like "fundamentalism" and "evangelical" to refer only to their religious ideology.

American Nationalism

We need to differentiate causes from symptoms, and in each expression of "Christian" nationalism, the "Christian" symbolism is rhetoric to justify American nationalism more than it is an expression of any biblically based teaching of Christian doctrine.

By whatever name, this movement has at its core the worldview of American exceptionalism—the idea that America is distinct, and, of course, superior to other countries. What makes American nationalism "Christian" is its claim that American superiority is divinely established. It also posits that only Christians (of a certain ideology) are "true Americans." It is reactionary in wanting to "take back" the United States for their God, which overlaps with the MAGA movement's embrace of Trump.

The basic American nationalist worldview is that the good can be achieved and maintained only by a hierarchical structure of concentrated power. The movement is inherently reactionist, no matter how much power it gains. Its Calvinist dualism defines the world in terms of a circle of ethical consideration. We all view the world and people in it in that way—we all have ethical blind spots that exclude some, and perhaps many, people from recognition of their worth. What American nationalism does is canonize and dogmatize the circle of ethical consideration to include white evangelical Americans and exclude others.

Since I keep referring back to the Calvinist version of the Christian religion, why am I also continually differentiating American nationalism from Christianity? The movement can be considered religious in the broad sense of the term, but nationalism in the United States is secular Calvinism—a civil religion. Some background will help explain why.

American nationalism has a long history, arguably as old as the United States itself. In 1967, Robert N. Bellah identified America's civil religion. It is, he argued, a national faith that exists alongside of and rather clearly differentiated from the churches and synagogues and that "has its own seriousness and integrity and requires the same care in understanding that any other religion does."[105]

Bellah showed that the American civil religion is patterned at every point after biblical archetypes—Americans are the chosen people brought out of the Old World into the promised land. But, he says, it is genuinely American and genuinely new with its own prophets and martyrs, sacred events and sacred places, brought together with its own solemn rituals and symbols. However, it is a religion that, he says, "has often been used and is being used today as a cloak for petty interests and ugly passions."[106]

Leilah Danielson argues that Bellah's concept of "civil religion" should be called "nationalism," offering similar arguments to what I have made here. However, Danielson unfairly accused Bellah of "inventing [with his idea of civil religion] a past that did not really exist, or that had existed only for white Protestants."[107]

---

[105] Bellah, 1.
[106] Bellah 19.
[107] Leilah Danielson, "Civil Religion as Myth, Not History," *Religions* (2019) *10*(6), 374. https://www.mdpi.com/2077-1444/10/6/374.

But that's the point that we need to take from American history. That past of solemn rituals and symbols didn't include many other Americas, as Danielson states, but it *did* exist in the minds of white Protestants. Bellah and Danielson each grasp part of the historical reality. America does have a civil religion, and, yes, it is biased in its whiteness and its Calvinism, but it is real and deeply formative for the attitudes of American nationalism.

The power structure of secular Calvinism is dualistic in its division between "real" Americans and the "others." That this power structure with its value delusions, petty interests, and ugly passions has long excluded Americans is central to American history. Yes, as Danielson says, we should tell the rest of the many stories of real Americans marginalized by secular Calvinism, but to explain the American right wing, we need to tell the story of its civil religion. Telling it is not endorsing it.

American nationalism *is* history, a history that is part selective memory by white Protestants but importantly also part the driving force of America's discrimination and exclusion. We can use the concept of civil religion today not as something to which we should aspire as the right wing uses it but as the ressentiment-fueled reactionism that has long spurred right-wing political action.

The myth of the United States as a shining city on a hill divinely established for white Calvinists was a story that evolved over many decades. The nationalist catechism taught children about America's prophets, most notably George Washington and Abraham Lincoln. It also taught the story of America's Manifest Destiny. God had led the chosen people out of Northern Europe to the "empty" wilderness to set the white man free in the promised land.

But the myth was more about the nation being for white people, the myth evolving over time as to who was white. The indigenous people were never white; they were savages who didn't deserve the land that they had failed to develop properly.[108] The African people who were captured, forcibly repatriated, and enslaved were never white and never could be. The Irish were not fully white until they weren't as undesirable as the Italians and Eastern Europeans who were not fully white until they weren't as undesirable as the Hispanics, and so on. The conception of who was undesirable changed, but what remained constant was the reality of the two-tiered society. America was for the white man—especially the white business man who could capitalize on the natural resources and cheap immigrant labor, applying the Calvinist worldview to secular matters.

The United States being on the winning side of multiple wars, including the two world wars, added weight to the myth of American moral and power superiority. It expanded the myth to now include the notion that the United States was the leader of the free world. The rest of the world needed the help and protection of the United States and its superior culture. That World War II was fought to defeat white nationalism was completely lost on believers in America's white nationalism.

After World War II, America practiced a sly form of settler colonialism throughout the world—extending American interests under the label of spreading democracy. America was great, and the rest of the world either looked up to America or hated its freedom.

Then the myth began to crumble. American nationalists had always grumbled about immigrants and minorities. It had always violently oppressed Black people. But after the legal victories of the Civil Rights Movement and the ascendancy of subcultures and intersectional feelings of the 1960s, the grumblings began to become rumblings.

Believers in the myth of America being for white people were now confronted with legal and social demands to treat others as equals. After President Richard Nixon's Watergate

---

[108] *Smithsonian American Art Museum*, "Manifest Destiny and Indian Removal," February 2015, https://americanexperience.si.edu/wp-content/uploads/2015/02/Manifest-Destiny-and-Indian-Removal.pdf.

scandal destroyed the myth of presidential inviolability and the loss of the Vietnam War destroyed the myth of the invincibility of American power, conservatives and American nationalists knew it was time for radical action.

We have to grant to the right wing that they possess the virtues of patience and planning to a much greater degree than those on the left wing. Conservatives drew up plans on how to reassert the myths of America's civil religion, especially those aspects that favored the interests of the wealthy. The conservative Heritage Foundation was created in 1973 and the libertarian Cato Institute in 1974, both to advance business interests under the banner of returning to traditional American values. Also notable were the founding of the Conservative Caucus in 1974, the Eagle Forum in 1972, and the Moral Majority in 1979, each also devoted to promoting traditional American values. Dozens of other advocacy groups followed, and all with the long-term goal of reasserting American exceptionalism and nationalism. Their efforts have been influential to US politics, government, and the public sphere to this day.

All of these right-wing political groups share in common the desire for a two-tiered society in which power is concentrated in a particular segment of society. Concentration of power is the motivation for right-wing political action as I detailed in my previous book.[109] The right wing is not against large government or an intrusive government *if* that large and/or intrusive government is enforcing their value delusions. The right wing—religious and secular—seeks a two-tiered society that concentrates power in the tier in which they reside and that grants them the benefits of the power structure. Whether the division in society is made along secular or religious lines is ultimately unimportant.

---

[109] Giles, *Left Wing, Right Wing*, 55f.

Lurching Toward Trump

Why does the religious Right embrace Trump? Because he is willing to embrace the worship of power. He is willing to go onstage at right-wing gatherings and hug and fondle the America flag like it is a stuffed animal or perhaps a fetish object. If Trump has a religion, it is most likely that which Stewart dubs power worship. In American nationalism, whether religious or secular, power is the structure of the two-tiered society that gives preference to the deserving people—the good and pure Americans.

But the acceptance of Trump as the focal point for American nationalism needed a good 40 years of preparation, even if the ground in the united States was already fertile for it. By the late 1970s, the movement to reclaim American nationalism needed a spokesman and a political figurehead. Some thought they had found it in Ronald Reagan, whose rise to the presidency coincided with the rise of the Moral Majority. Reagan, being an actor, knew how to present himself. But Reagan proved to be too practical. He was right wing but remained more grounded in a pragmatic conservatism and the rule of law.

American nationalism needed something more. Bush, Sr., didn't fit the bill, nor did many other right-wing politicians in the 1990s. Newt Gingrich did. His Contract with America legislative agenda was a right-wing dream come true, seemingly a culmination of two decades of conservative maneuvering. When Gingrich led Republicans to a landslide victory in the 1994 congressional election over a Democratic establishment wracked by corruption scandals, he was able to change the political landscape. Gingrich turned American politics into a polarized war of good Americans against traitorous, sick, corrupt Democrats.[110] His extreme rhetoric combined themes from American exceptionalism and the religious Right. House Speaker Gingrich was speaking the

---

[110] Sam Rosenfeld, *The Polarizers* (University of Chicago Press, 2017).

language of the ressentiment-fueled reactionaries, and he unlocked the door for openly combative politics.

Unfortunately, for American nationalists, Gingrich was too combative and too dictatorial, ending up alienating his own Republican caucus, who forced him out of the speakership after four years. The editorial board of *The New York Times* described Gingrich as "an expert in how to seize power, but a novice in holding it."[111] That was the opinion in November 1998, when the editors of a major newspaper thought that Gingrich was a too "radical [and] polarizing figure to last in leadership." But that was 1998, and Gingrich had succeeded in pushing the boundaries of political extremism. What was radical rhetoric then is normal now.

A new spokesman was needed. Bush, Jr., also was not a good figurehead, though his "global war on terror" certainly helped buttress American exceptionalism.[112] Bush's war was readily seen as a war against Islam, and "Christian" nationalism had a useful way to frame their version of American superiority. America projected its miliary might abroad, renewing with fresh fervor the extension of American interests under the label of spreading democracy. The domestic increase in surveillance and curtailment of civil liberties, such as in the Patriot Act, was a boon for those wanting to strengthen the United States' two-tiered society and concentration of power in the government. America was still the shining city on the hill, but with security cameras pointing down at everyone.

But then a skinny Black man with a funny name got elected president. This fact galvanized the reactionaries, even more than did the "global war on terror." Few politicians have been the target of more vicious rhetoric and conspiracy

---

[111] "The Gingrich Coup," *The New York Times*, November 7, 1998, https://www.nytimes.com/1998/11/07/opinion/the-gingrich-coup.html.
[112] "Global War on Terror," *George W. Bush Presidential Library*, accessed July 11, 2024, https://www.georgewbushlibrary.gov/research/topic-guides/global-war-terror.

theories than was Barack Obama during his presidency.[113] Obama had promised to reduce the partisanship in government that had plagued it since Gingrich. Whether Obama was effective or not at reaching out to Republicans, it was immediately clear that Republicans were having none of it; their political agenda turned to opposing Obama as its first priority.[114] Obstruction and partisan division took over Washington.

And the mainline Republicans were nice to Obama compared to the reactionary rank and file, which went apocalyptic in bemoaning the "tragedy" of President Obama.[115] The election of a Black man as president (half-Black is all-Black in the eyes of a white supremacist) struck at the heart of American white nationalism. It was easier to believe the conspiracy theories that Obama was a foreign Manchurian candidate who would open the US borders to al-Qaeda and turn the country into a Muslim caliphate than to believe that a plurality of Americans was willing to vote for a half-Black man for president. A cottage industry of right-wing bloggers, influencers, and con(spiracy) artists sprang up. Professionals and amateurs formed the Obama hate machine attacking the president in a breadth and ferocity the country had never seen.[116]

The Obama hate machine was, in brief, a juxtaposition and even culmination of trends from right-wing America. The long simmering jingoism of American exceptionalism that had

---

[113] Michael Barkun, "Conspiracy Theories about Barack Obama," in *A Culture of Conspiracy* (University of California Press, 2013).

[114] Frank James, "Sen. Mitch McConnell Insists: One and Done for Obama," *It's All Politics: NPR*, November 4, 2020, https://www.npr.org/sections/itsallpolitics/2010/11/04/131069048/sen-mcconnell-insists-one-term-for-obama.

[115] The Southern Poverty Law Center, "In Their Words: Hating Barack Obama," *Fighting Hate*, 2015, https://www.splcenter.org/fighting-hate/intelligence-report/2015/their-words-hating-barack-obama.

[116] Bill Press, *The Obama Hate Machine: The Lies, Distortions, and Personal Attacks on the President—and Who Is Behind Them* (Thomas Dunne Books, 2012).

been stimulated by the combination of conservative efforts to revive American nationalism in the 1970s and Gingrich's pushing of the boundaries of political extremism in the 1990s now had its ultimate target. Obama's election became a catalyst for anti-Black and anti-Muslim bigotry and enhanced the presence of anti-immigrant rhetoric and "Christian" rhetoric of American nationalism.

The rise of social media during Obama's two terms—then candidate Obama was the first to announce his vice presidential pick on Twitter—leant itself to fast, lazy thinking and easy rhetorical attacks. Reactionaries could spew their hate from the comfort of their own homes instantly to everyone all over the country. Social media's hormone-stimulating feedback of upvotes and likes encouraged open expression but also encouraged focusing on quantity over quality of expression. American nationalism, especially its dark side, could scale up its reach, and its ideas reached more people. The bigoted underworld of ressentiment now had its biggest ever platform.

Despite all the rhetoric and breathless conspiracy theories predicting that Obama would destroy America, it didn't happen. Obama's presidency was not at all radical. Obama turned out to be far less left wing than anyone thought he would be. That reality had no affect on the Obama hate machine. The narrative was set—Obama was ruining America. That narrative was too useful to the demagogues, too profitable for the bloggers and con(spiracy) theorists, to let go of. The hatred for Obama had connected the branches of the right-wing subculture as nothing previously had, and tools of the Internet and social media made reactionary political activism more robust, efficient, and widespread.

It was this environment into which Trump walked. Give him credit—he sensed the opportunity and took advantage of it. Trump was already well practiced at creating a television mirage of his own competency and authority.[117] He simply turned that into a mirage of competency and authority about how Obama and Democrats were destroying America, added a thick helping of good old-fashioned anti-immigrant rhetoric, and *voilà*.

Perhaps Trump was so out there, so willing to take down the political guardrails of political decorum in his nationalist rhetoric, that his atheistic shortcomings could be overlooked. For the "Christian" nationalists, Trump doesn't need to be Christian, and he doesn't need to be a moral person. To be their political figurehead, he just needs to say he hates the same people and things that they hate.

The United States has always had a hard-Right wing seeking a two-tiered society. For example, before World War II, the United States had a branch of Germany's Nazi party, the German American Bund. Its zenith was a 1939 Nuremberg-style rally of 20,000 supporters at Madison Square Garden in New York City. A movie of the rally, still existing today, shows Nazi swastikas side by side with American flags, and center stage, an enormous portrait of George Washington portrayed in his military uniform, his whole body surrounded by a white light as though he was about to ascend into heaven.[118]

Religious symbolism is never far away in nationalist movements. Now, the American nationalists create pictures of Trump bathed in white light surrounded by American flags. America's civil religion has found its new messiah.

---

[117] Ramin Setoodeh, *Apprentice in Wonderland: How Donald Trump and Mark Burnett Took America Through the Looking Glass* (Harper, 2024).

[118] Emily Bruder, "When 20,000 American Nazis Descended Upon New York City," *The Atlantic*, October 10, 2017, https://www.theatlantic.com/video/index/542499/marshall-curry-nazi-rally-madison-square-garden-1939/.

12. Making America Victims Again (and Always)

Equipped with a broader knowledge of US history, let's address our central question of why some people support Trump. It's not really about Trump, as should be apparent by now, but, of course, Trump is the current focal point, spokesman, and political figurehead of the American nationalist movement, so what about Trump?

What's the point of Trump? Why does he say and do what he says and does? What's the point of supporting him? People do things for reasons. "Why?" is always a good question to ask.

Trump's reasons are obvious. He shows again and again that he craves and needs to be the center of attention.[119] He also seems to really like feeling important.[120] Those who support and even idolize Trump also seem to get feelings of importance from doing so. That's common human behavior. People frequently join groups and/or become fans of public figures to gain a sense of importance and identity—think Swifties.

There is, though, a particular strain of importance and identity that the MAGA people are feeling and expressing in their adoration of Trump. Their group is different from, for example, fans of pop music acts or sports teams.

The religious undertones of the MAGA movement are heavily present, following the pattern of American nationalism's civil religion. Those undertones led commentators to view some Trump rallies as being rituals of the "Church of Trump," in which, "Trump's audience is his congregation, and the former president their pastor."[121]

---

[119] Ted Anthony, "Love him? Hate him? For Donald Trump, Attention Is Attention," *Associated Press*, April 4, 2023, https://apnews.com/article/trump-attention-indictment-arraignment-president-1e87be51004b12dc7b85728fd7946b56.

[120] Ali Velshi, "President Trump: My People Should Give Me the Attention Kim Jong Un Gets," *MSNBC*, June 15, 2018, https://www.youtube.com/watch?v=7q7SoqhCzCA.

Certainly, the many "Jesus is my savior, Trump is my president" hats and shirts worn by people who support Trump gives the impression that this is a religious movement if not a Church of Trump.[122]

But what is this pseudoreligion about? Those who support Trump may believe he shares their Calvinist values, though again there is little reason to believe that Trump has any religious beliefs or practices. Some might say that Trump is milking all of this for his own personal aggrandizement. But even if Trump is a narcissist, as for years some commentators have claimed,[123] that doesn't explain why people support Trump. People do things for reasons, usually because they believe they are receiving something valuable in return for doing so. What are supporters of Trump getting out of it?

Trump Is a Focal Point, But a Focus for What?

A key characteristic of the MAGA movement is that it is antagonistic and externally focused. Sure, there's a lot of "yay, rah, Trump; yay, rah, us!" but the MAGA movement is dominated by the reactionary feeling of *we are under threat!*"

The constant rhetoric of American nationalism has always been that America is under threat. In the first years of the United States, that was true—there was a military threat

---

[121] Michael C. Bender, "The Church of Trump: How He's Infusing Christianity into His Movement," *New York Times*, April 1, 2024, https://www.nytimes.com/2024/04/01/us/politics/trump-2024-religion.html.

[122] Peter Smith, "Jesus Is Their Savior, Trump Is Their Candidate. Ex-president's Backers Say He Shares Faith, Values," *Associated Press*, May 18, 2024, https://apnews.com/article/trump-christian-evangelicals-conservatives-2024-election-43f25118c133170c77786daf316821c3.

[123] Jeffrey Kluger, "The Truth About Donald Trump's Narcissism," *Time*, August 11, 2015, https://time.com/3992363/trump-narcissism/.
Bill Eddy, "Malignant Narcissism: Does the President Really Have It?" *High Conflict Institute*, March 19,2019, https://highconflictinstitute.com/personality-disorders/malignant-narcissism-does-the-president-really-have-it/.

from Great Britain, but by the mid-1800s that threat had receded. The Civil War was, on both sides, seen as a threat, with good reason, and much of the mythic language of American nationalism was honed during this period. Then there has been the overarching feeling that new immigrants are a threat to the purity of white America.

Reactionism is a strong component of American nationalism. In Chapter 3, I defined reactionism as the response to and the reaction against increased diversity and inclusion in society—the dread fear that somewhere someone you feel is your inferior is being recognized as your equal. Reactionaries see diversity as a threat. They believe that the purity of the traditional order is being corrupted by the presence of others. The Calvinist belief system is also suffused with such feelings of "we are under threat!" and this explains why there is overlap and borrowing between American nationalism and Calvinism.

MAGA is a reactionary movement, overlapping with and borrowing from American nationalism and Calvinism. What "MAGA" really means is "we think America is *not* great." We can listen to MAGA adherents and let them tell us who they feel is making America not great, and those people are who the MAGA adherents feel is a threat to them and their perceived purity of America's traditional order. Feeling under threat means feeling someone is out to get you, and people in the MAGA movement are not shy about who they feel is out to get them, America, and their little dog, too.

One of the most telling trends in MAGA has been a common conspiracy theory about the perceived threat of critical race theory (CRT), even when it isn't being taught in public schools. MAGA people apparently feel very, very threatened by CRT, and they are usually straw manning it as a war on white people,[124] a war on Christianity,[125] or hidden

---

[124] Douglas Murray and Lex Fridman, "War on White People," June 22, 2022, https://www.youtube.com/watch?v=FJlRJ-1kgqw.
[125] Robert Downen, "At Texas GOP Convention, Republicans Call for Spiritual

Marxism.[126] When pressed to give a more rational reason why they want to ban all mention of CRT (and Black history, especially slavery and segregation), they accuse CRT of trying to relegate Black people to being perpetual victims.[127]

The MAGA reactionary sentiment against CRT quickly morphs into accusations that allowing discussion of the history of racial discrimination, including the historical reality of American slavery, harms whites. The reactionaries need to attack CRT to redeem America's racial contract[128]—a social contract that, as Charles W. Mills observed, is a power hierarchy that favors white people.[129]

All of this panic over CRT is being expressed because MAGA people are claiming to be victims of CRT. And they are victims not just of CRT, the MAGA people are claiming to be victims also of wokeness, the gay agenda, immigrants, and having to pay taxes. (I left out a few dozen other boogeymen allegedly preying on the poor MAGA victims.)

The MAGA movement is the reactionary Right crying "circle the wagons, the savages are attacking!" The name of the game is victimhood. It is a chronic state of feeling one is a victim of conspiracies—the "they are out to get me" dimension of the conspiracy theorist.

Trump, craving attention, exploits the reactionary Right's craving for victimhood—something at which he is very good. In his public appearances, "I'm a victim," is a frequent

---

Warfare," *The Texas Tribune*, May 28, 2024, https://www.texastribune.org/2024/05/28/texas-gop-convention-elections-religion-delegates-platform/.

[126] Heritage Action for America, "Reject Critical Race Theory," accessed June 25, 2024, https://heritageaction.com/toolkit/rejectcrt.

[127] Marsha Blackburn, "Why Is Critical Race Theory Dangerous for Our Kids?" July 21, 2021, https://www.blackburn.senate.gov/2021/7/why-is-critical-race-theory-dangerous-for-our-kids.

[128] Marissa Jackson Sow, "Whiteness as Guilt: Attacking Critical Race Theory to Redeem the Racial Contract," *UCLA Law Review*, March 29, 2022, https://www.uclalawreview.org/whiteness-as-guilt-attacking-critical-race-theory-to-redeem-the-racial-contract/.

[129] Charles W. Mills, *The Racial Contract* (Cornell University Press, 1997).

refrain for Trump, though he probably believes it. Trump and MAGA have a symbiotic relationship of call and response in their victimhood and reactionism.

Is the boisterous vehemence of Trump and his minions best understood as a demand for recognition of their victimhood? Is that what the culture wars are really about? Does all the reactionary rhetoric boil down to "You can't talk about social injustices against minorities, because *we* are the greater victims here!" This demand would explain the motivation for much of what the MAGA martyrs say and do.

Victimhood Culture

According to the Paris Institute for Critical Thinking, victimhood is a common response to felt trauma, real or imagined, and a sense of victimhood can undermine assumptions about the world as a just and reasonable place.[130] Claiming victimhood, the institute says, can also work as a strategy to avoid responsibility and criticism, producing a "victim mentality." Taking on that mentality of victimhood, one can feel above ethical accountability yet entitled to render ethical judgment on others. Victimhood is a version of ressentiment and its feelings of impotence and despising.

Sociologists Bradley Campbell and Jason Manning argue that there is a rise of a "victimhood culture" that incentivizes people to publicize grievances and make victimhood a central part of their identity.[131] It is, they say, a dizzying cultural milieu that replaces a culture of dignity with a culture of identifying as a victim. Trump is a leading voice in victimhood culture, and MAGA supporters are eager participants.

---

[130] Carlo Salzani, "Victimhood: Editorial Note," *dePICTions volume 4 (2024): Victimhood*, Paris Institute for Critical Thinking, https://parisinstitute.org/editorial-note-iv/.

[131] Bradley Campbell and Jason Manning, *The Rise of Victimhood Culture: Microaggressions, Safe Spaces, and the New Culture Wars* (Palgrave Macmillan, 2018).

Victimhood is a strange way to feel important, but it is not an uncommon expression of ressentiment. Some subcultures are oriented toward commiserating over their perceived victimhood and take on an attitude of "us against the world" as a source of identity.[132] The MAGA subculture is hardly alone in this behavior, but a whataboutery of "that group plays the victim, too" doesn't change the reality that the MAGA movement is fundamentally an expression of victimhood. True, "cancel culture" coming from the left wing is also a "victim mentality." Trump and people in the MAGA movement are another version of "cancel culture." As Campbell and Manning observe, there is now a clash between these two cancel cultures trying to out-victim each other.

Since being indicted multiple times for multiple alleged crimes, Trump has greatly accelerated his claims of victimhood. All accusations against him are witch hunts, an egregious miscarriage of justice in which he is the victim of a vast conspiracy.[133] Biden, the Justice Department, Democrats, and the Wicked Witch are all out to get him. That's why he needs money, so he says. It's all part of his political campaign, of course.[134] As I was writing this paragraph, news broke that Trump claimed he was "tortured" while being booked, fingerprinted, and photographed because of his State of Georgia criminal indictment in August 2023. Trump's claim that he was the victim of torture came in a fundraising email selling mugs with his arrest mug shot.[135]

---

[132] Giles, *Rethinking Misrecognition*, 252–253.

[133] Hyemin Han, "Debunking Trump's Witch Hunt Theory," *Lawfare*, June 16, 2023, https://www.lawfaremedia.org/article/debunking-trump-s-witch-hunt-theory.

[134] "Trump turns New York fraud trial into campaign stop, 'a witch hunt,'" *France24*, March 10, 2023, https://www.france24.com/en/americas/20231003-trump-turns-new-york-fraud-trial-into-campaign-stop-a-witch-hunt.

[135] Robert Tait, "Trump Mocked For Claiming He Was 'Tortured' In Georgia Mugshot Arrest," *The Guardian*, June 25, 2024, https://www.theguardian.com/us-news/article/2024/jun/25/trump-tortured-georgia-arrest-mugshot.

People who support him are apparently still willing to shell out money to help Victim Trump, who is claiming he is being martyred for them. It is one thing to proclaim one's innocence, but Trump spins a conspiracy theory that "the radical left Democrats, Marxists, communists, and fascists" are out to get him.[136] Sidney Blumenthal commented that Trump's conspiracy theories about legal persecution is a quasi-religious mythology of martyrdom. Blumenthal concludes that "[Trump's] celebrity has been transformed into a passion play of victimization."[137]

Are the people who support Victim Trump themselves victims? They say they are, even if they don't use the v-word. Their victimhood is an expression of their ressentiment, their feelings of their own impotence. They feel that America is not great and that they are under threat—victims of the rest of society that is destroying America's purity.

They have the right to free speech and to voice their political grievances. We should listen to their complaints and ask them two questions. One, are your complaints justified, and are you actually victimized by those you claim are threatening you (CRT, wokeness, the gay agenda, immigrants, and so on)? Two, are you seeking a positive solution, wallowing in your victimhood, or reveling in being hostile to soothe your feelings of victimhood?

If Trump and people in the MAGA movement can justify their complaints and accusations and show that they are willing to work for solutions cooperatively and constructively, then we owe them our respect and cooperation. However, if they are instead interested only in complaining, interested

---

[136] Peter Wade, "Trump Honored as 'Man of Decade,' Tells Crowd: 'I'm Being Indicted for You,'" *Rolling Stone*, June 25, 2023, https://www.rollingstone.com/politics/politics-news/trump-indicted-consider-it-great-badge-of-honor-1234777874/.

[137] Sidney Blumenthal, "Trump's Legal Woes Are Part of His Quasi-religious Mythology of Martyrdom," *The Guardian*, August 21, 2024, https://www.theguardian.com/commentisfree/2023/aug/21/trump-election-giuliani-sidney-blumenthal.

only in making accusations, spreading conspiracy theories, and attacking and canceling other people, then they are ultimately victimizing themselves. They are showing they aren't trying to make America great; they are trying to make themselves even greater victims.

The Ressentiment of the War on Woke

One target of reactionaries' victimhood claims is worthy of deeper exploration because it will lead to deeper insights into why people support Trump and into the wider movement of American nationalism. That target is the ubiquitous but ghostly "woke" or "wokeness" that reactionaries allege to be a threat to the purity of America.

Ron DeSantis made a "war on woke" the core crusade of his presidential campaign.[138] He didn't unseat Trump as the Republican front-runner for the party's nomination, but not because his opposition to wokeness has been unpopular among the right-wing reactionaries.

What "woke" means to reactionaries like DeSantis is less than clear. They certainly aren't using the term in its original positive sense.[139] Sometimes it seems to be reactionaries' new slang term for "liberal," and its use as an insult or angry meme is usually directed at ambiguous conspiracies and groups.

Definitely, "woke" appears to signify something hated and feared by right-wingers, who fight a culture war against it. Their accusations of "wokeness" are flailing at an obscure enemy, lashing out at an ethereal foe. Angry antiwoke memes shared among right-wingers are mostly inside jokes mocking the mysterious "woke crowd." The talk of "wokeness" seems

---

[138] David Smith, "Ron DeSantis Put Nearly All His Eggs In The Basket Of A 'War On Woke,'" *The Guardian*, January 22, 2024, https://www.theguardian.com/us-news/2024/jan/21/ron-desantis-republican-presidential-candidate-dropped-out-analysis.

[139] NAACP, "Reclaiming the Word "Woke" as Part of African American Culture," 2023, https://naacp.org/resources/reclaiming-word-woke-part-african-american-culture.

mostly a type of internal propaganda disseminated among the right-wing subculture to stoke fear and create unity against an enemy.

The right wing has been doing this kind of finger pointing for a very long time—targeting minorities, immigrants, and others as threats to American purity. It is as if the right wing, in order to keep existing, needs to talk constantly about enemies, and wokeness is the new enemy.

Or maybe it's the old enemy with a new right-wing marketing label. The memes about wokeness target the usual subjects of reactionary ressentiment: women, minorities, nonheteronormative people, workers' rights activists, and so on. New wine in old wine bottles? Old *whines* in new memes?

Before we dismiss wokeness as just another propaganda ploy, let's ask if anything in the world has changed. The new antiwoke propaganda memes of the past few years may be a reaction to something new.

Right-wing antiwoke memes and insults arose concurrently with two significant social events. One was the Me Too movement (2006–present), in which women spoke more openly against being sexually harassed and assaulted. Another was the Black Lives Matter movement (2013–present), in which Black people spoke more openly against being assaulted and murdered by police and others. Two separate movements with the same message: Stop oppressing us; we have rights.

Public movements of women and Blacks standing up for themselves seem to have really bothered right-wingers. The predominant themes of antiwoke declarations are protests that women and Black people are complaining unreasonably about oppression.

It's eerily reminiscent of the anti-politically correct (anti-PC) propaganda of the 1990s, in particular the Gingrich years. Like with their current use of "wokeness," right-wingers had no clear definition of "PC," but it nevertheless was touted as a threat to America's traditional cultural order. For over 30 years, an "anti-PC stance and continual stream of non-PC statements both online and in-person has been much of former President Donald Trump's appeal since his initial candidacy in 2015."[140] It makes sense to understand antiwokeness as a new version of anti-PC, a new version of ressentiment.

Many antiwoke statements and memes revolve around anger that other people are pointing out bigotry and structural discrimination. Antiwoke memes on social media are attempts to mock away the reality of bigotry and ridicule anyone who is aware of that reality. Among pundits and politicians, antiwoke statements are part of a strategy claiming the "woke crowd" are denying reality.

> The new era of American conservatism, largely defined by Trump, has reframed PC as a threat to our national security by claiming that it makes us blind to terrorism and the inherently violent nature of specific ethnic groups, particularly Islamic Middle Easterners, as well as Central and South Americans.[141]

The message of the propaganda is that people who are not white are a threat to Americans and America and that wokeness (activists against discrimination) is a denial of that threat. Therefore, wokeness is anti-American—an evil attitude held by people who hate facts and truth.

The "war on woke" is propaganda disseminated among the right wing to stoke fear and create unity against an enemy—an old enemy redefined. "Corruption" for the right wing is about cultural purity not ethics or law. If wokeness is "the quality of being alert to injustice and discrimination in

---

[140] Andrew F. Baird, J. Micah Roos, and J. Scott Carter, "Understanding the Rise of Anti-Political Correctness Sentiment: The Curious Role of Education," *Humanity & Society* Volume 47, Issue 1, September 1, 2021, https://journals.sagepub.com/doi/full/10.1177/01605976221120536#bibr27-01605976221120536.

[141] Michèle Lamont, Bo Yun Park, and Elena Ayala-Hurtado, "Trump's Electoral Speeches and His Appeal to the American White Working Class," *The British Journal of Sociology* 68(S1):S153–S180, 2017.

society, especially racism,"[142] then people having such an alertness or awareness are a danger to and corruption of the traditional order and power structure. Those who wish to preserve those power structures certainly see the awareness of injustice and discrimination as a threat.

To counter the alleged threat of wokeness, reactionaries try to turn the tables. Wokeness is the real discrimination—a plot to harm America by attacking white people. The other part of this reality reversal is the portrayal of being antiwoke as a defense of tradition and heritage. This admittedly has a grain of truth because the antiwoke crowd are defending America's tradition and heritage of structural inequality and oppression.

Yes, some people are aware of the reality of entrenched bigotry in human society. Yes, the number of those people so aware is increasing. What could be the motivation of anyone who wants to stop people from being aware of and talking about these irrefutable facts?

The history of human bigotry and structural oppression is real. And those who respond to that with cries of "you are attacking America" are protesting too much. The reality of human bigotry and structural oppression is the turd of history. No matter how much you polish up the turd with talk of tradition and heritage, it's still a turd. Trying to cancel discussion of that turd doesn't make it not a turd.

It is no surprise that Trump exploits the reactionaries' unease and ressentiment over the increased awareness of America's history of injustice. Antiwoke is a strain of reactionism of people who feel they are under siege and even oppressed by changing social norms and demographic shifts.

---

[142] "Wokeness," *Ecosia powered by Oxford Languages*, accessed June 25, 2024, https://www.ecosia.org/search?q=wokeness. Also, "a state of being aware, especially of social problems such as racism and inequality," "Wokeness," *Cambridge English Dictionary*, accessed June 25, 2024, https://dictionary.cambridge.org/us/dictionary/english/wokeness.

In the reactionary worldview, white Calvinists are the victims of oppression from wokeness. Reactionaries desire to keep others in their place—powerless and silent. Reactionaries can call on the vibrant symbolism of Calvinism and American nationalism to defend the traditional order in which they reside and from which they benefit. They feel the need to take back their country and make it great again—greatness defined as the purity of the past hierarchical power structure that existed before marginalized people could participate equally in the public sphere.

Trump speaks this language of victimhood and ressentiment. Reactionaries can see him as the focal point of their ressentiment against formally marginalized people who are becoming increasingly empowered. The MAGA movement is the latest adaptation of American nationalism, modified to the issues of this century, but still clinging fiercely to the Calvinist dualism of American nationalism.

13. The Big Lie—Desire Versus the Law

No discussion of why people support Trump can neglect to include the January 6 attack on the US Capitol Building. Ressentiment and victimhood can motivate people to action, and that is what the world witnessed that day. On this issue, too, the question of what motivated the attack is not about Trump, although here Trump was the leading voice of it.

It's fairly easy to understand why someone who has lost an election would be upset about it—and yes, as for the facts, there is zero evidence at any level that the election in 2020 was stolen away from Trump. It's easy to understand why someone who has lost, someone who didn't get what they want, would want that not to be the case and would want to win instead. That's normal human desire.

It is the actions that Trump took that are at issue here. Trump can say whatever he wants, Trump can believe whatever he wants, and he can lie if he wants. The reality is that he lost the election. Whether he acted to try to overturn those results, whether he actually did commit treason, because that's really the question—treason—is up to a jury to decide.

Beliefs and Desires

My question, as a philosopher who tries to understand the causes of injustice, is why Trump's supporters believe the lie that the election was stolen. Why would a human being believe something against all evidence to the contrary?

One of the central traits of we human beings is that we have free will. And of course, having free will means we are free to make mistakes. We are finite, fallible beings, and we make mistakes because we sometimes use our free will to choose the wrong path, make the wrong decision. We very often will let our desires overcome what is in front of us—the evidence that's clearly in front of us. Philosopher René

Descartes said that when the will is allowed to rush ahead of the intellect, we can make mistakes.[143] His overly simplistic answer was just to rein in the will and let the intellect rule. Ironically, that was Descartes asserting his desire for simplicity over how complicated things actually are.

Our intellect is powerful, but it is not an oracle. It's a tool. Intellect and logic are valuable tools that can be used to reach the truth about matters. The problem is that the tool of the intellect can also be used to deny what's real and true.

Throughout human history, people in power have used their power to convince other people to use their intellect to justify belief in falsehoods. We usually correctly refer to this as manipulating people's emotions or playing on their emotions. But too often missed in that discussion is that people in power are exploiting people's emotions to get them to channel their *intellect* toward certain beliefs.

Because we are beings who need to anchor our sense of self in a sense of meaning, there is a very natural impulse, when the law or reality goes against our desires, to wish for that law or reality to change and the results to change. When your sports team loses, you wish that your sports team had won instead. When your party or candidate loses an election, you wish that that hadn't happened.

Trump had the very human—childish but human nevertheless—desire not to have lost the election. His followers who voted for him and supported him for whatever their reasons desired that he had not lost the election. Desiring those things is very human—that's okay. Wishing that things weren't the way they are—that's okay, and sometimes a very positive thing.

But using your intellect and your free will to try to assert your desires over the law, over what is real, that's where the problems begin. That's where injustices start. Trump is in no

---

[143] René Descartes, *Discourse on the Method of Rightly Conducting One's Reason and of Seeking Truth*. Project Gutenberg. http://www.gutenberg.org/ebooks/59.

way new. He is not entirely unique. His followers aren't new. This is not a unique phenomenon. The Big Lie is the latest manifestation of reactionary desire—the biggest and most egregious political lie *so far*.

Exploiting Desires

History records many instances of people in power playing on people's emotions to get them to believe intellectually something that's not true. I say these are the causes of injustice. The injustices that we see time and again are when one group of people who have the power to act on their desires go on to deny the law and reality in a way that denies the realities and rights of other people. That's the core of injustice. It is desiring and intellectually rationalizing that your desires are more important than other people's realities.

I won't go into the specifics of the indictments against Trump, but one particular charge speaks very strongly to this. It's the charge of conspiracy against rights: to conspire to injure, oppress, threaten, or intimidate any person in the free exercise or enjoyment of their rights or privileges secured to them by the law. The legal theory from the prosecution is that Trump acted to conspire to deprive voters of their right to vote and have their votes count. In essence, that charge is saying that Trump intellectually justified his desire not to lose the election and acted to manipulate others to think and act similarly.[144]

Again, Trump can say what he wants, he can whine and pout and cry about his defeat. But if, as the indictment accuses him of having done, he did act to overturn the election, then that is depriving everyone who voted of their right to have

---

[144] Jaclyn Diaz, "The Charges Facing Trump in the Jan. 6 Investigation, Explained," *NPR*, August 2, 2023, https://www.npr.org/2023/08/01/1191493880/trump-january-6-charges-indictment-counts.

their vote counted because their votes being counted is guaranteed. It's the law; it's the reality.

You can't just say "my sports team lost; therefore, we're going to adjust the score so that my sports team won." You can't just say, "we lost the election; therefore, we'll just adjust the vote totals so that we won the election." You can't just say, "we don't like those people over there; therefore, we're going to ignore the law and discriminate against those people." It doesn't matter what political party someone belongs to— desire should not trump the law.

This conspiracy to deny rights is a legal concept, but it applies ethically to so much of what we do. The basic questions of ethics and law regard what rights human beings have, what privileges they have, and where those privileges and rights intersect with other individuals' privileges and rights. Certainly, how to balance everyone's rights is complicated and involves tricky questions, which is why philosophers and legal scholars continue to debate and discuss these questions. We as a society continue to evolve in our thinking about what rights human beings have and how we best balance the rights of individuals within the larger society.

Complexities aside, the basic issue is clear and sound. Do you have any right to deny the rights of others? No, of course not. And that is especially the case if the only basis for your actions is that you want it to be otherwise than how it is.

And yet, if you look at many of the injustices that people commit, you can ask two simple questions. Why did they do this? What were they trying to accomplish? I put it to you that you will find that the core cause and intention was the perpetrators' desire for their desires to be more important than other people's rights.

And when you question further as to why the perpetrator had this desire, you will find in almost every case of injustice that the perpetrator was trying to buttress their sense of self with a sense of meaning—a sense of meaning that comes at the cost of other people's rights and privileges and sometimes lives. If we turn all those questions onto ourselves, and look at our past actions, we will regrettably find that it's also true of us and the things that we have done that were unethical and unjust.

We all deserve to be recognized for who we are. We all deserve to have our desires, to have our sense of self—and a healthy sense of self. No one has the right to deny that to us or to anyone. That includes no one having the right to say to people who support Trump that they're not allowed to support him. Likewise, no one has the right to say to people who support Biden that they don't have the right to support him. Absolutely, no one has the right to act violently to overturn an election result. Neither side has any right to let their desires overcome the realities. But both sides do it anyway because, sadly, that's what human beings do.

We need to break that cycle.

14. How Do We Break the Cycle of Antagonistic Politics?

Ressentiment. Lazy thinking. Xenophobia. Jingoism. Victimhood. These are all aspects of why some people support Trump. Trump is not the leader of a movement but is a focal point for one. He is the latest focal point of a strain of political culture unique to the United States that we can identify as American nationalism.

Many have said, with justification, that American nationalism is dangerous and that the MAGA movement is its most dangerous incarnation yet. The dire warnings could be correct. Whether or not Trump and those who support him are the existential threat that some people claim, the rhetoric and hostility from the right wing has altered politics and all but obliterated political discourse.

If it was the right wing's intention to turn American politics into a Calvinist dualist battleground, they have succeeded. The United States currently has two political parties that, despite the fact that the majority of their political agendas is identical, act like they are in a titanic apocalyptic battle between good and evil, with both sides claiming to be the good and the other side evil. Both sides see any sign of cooperation as capitulation. In the arms race of hating and despising, the MAGA-controlled Republican Party may still be ahead, but the Democratic Party and its allies are determined to catch up.

Politics in the United States is antagonistic. To an extent, it always has been, but there's no question that the antagonism and aggression in politics are louder and more pervasive than ever. Numerous factors are to blame: corporate consolidation of news sources, unlimited big money donations that buy politicians and their legislative votes, and the indispensable wallpaper of the 24-hour news cycle.[145]

---

[145] Liane Hansen and David Folkenflik, "The Power of the 24-Hour News Cycle,"

It's been fashionable to blame social media for the increased antagonism—and I could cite dozens of commentators who cast that blame—but social media is a commercial product of larger forces, and the antagonism that saturates social media is a symptom of deeper human ressentiment. Social media didn't create ugliness, it only lifted up rotten floorboards and exposed the ugly side of human nature.

What social media has done, to serve its corporate owners' craving for profits, is not only to expose but especially to *promote* the ugly side of human nature. Antagonism keeps eyes on screens, and the corporate algorithms keep the antagonism simmering and the online hating and despising going. Social media is the new indispensable wallpaper of the public sphere, and it has replaced most other forms of political action.

It is reasonable for people to oppose the agenda of the right wing politically under whatever label it operates. But opposing Trump and those who support him with a mirror image of their lazy thinking and empty rhetoric is unhelpful. Shouting back at someone shouting at you is a natural instinct, but it is unproductive.

I'm not at all suggesting some saccharine sentiment of let's just talk with MAGA people. Of course sincere dialogue is good, but, to be honest, most of the people in the MAGA movement aren't interested. They won't read what we write, and they won't listen to what we say. To do so would go against their chosen identity of being warriors against evil, and they define us as evil.

So, what to do?

We should stand against that which we perceive to be evil. On that point, the Calvinists and all they have influenced are correct. Where they go wrong is in imagining good and evil as being black-and-white and thus easily discernable. Reality

NPR, May 29, 2005, https://www.npr.org/2005/05/29/4671485/the-power-of-the-24-hour-news-cycle.

is complex, and the simplistic dualism of Calvinism and similar ideologies fail to reflect the real world and our experiences and problems in it. Injustices are real and seldom can be rectified by the lazy thinking of dualism. Our thinking and actions in response to injustices must reflect the nuances and complexities of the factors that contribute to injustices.

We've tried disparaging, demeaning, diminishing, and even destroying political opponents for centuries. It's never made the world a better place for long. The answer to injustice is not to try to eliminate those you dislike. There probably isn't a simple answer for ending injustice. But if there is an answer, it lies far more in working with the laws of reality than in trying to assert our desires as law.

Three Forms of Politics

Elections and politics are expressions of human nature; human fears; human desires; and, of course, human society. Politics lends itself to conflict because politics is about power and a struggle for power. The problem, which is a very human problem, is that you want government to represent you and your interests, but other people want government to represent them and their interests, and their interests do not necessarily coincide with your interests.

Power is the foundational reality of politics. Everything else is built on that foundation, whether you are simply looking for better services from your government, sensible laws, social change, or someone to represent you in government to advocate for your interests.

We can identify three forms of politics with different approaches to power relations. The three forms reflect different orientations that people have toward power, politics, and political action.

Antagonistic Politics

One form is antagonistic politics, the form frequently discussed so far in this book. Politics is seldom devoid of conflict, but when political issues and the realities of other people are oversimplified, politics slides into antagonism. Many people see politics as a matter of "if I defeat somebody else, then I control the situation, and I can assert my interests over the interests of other people."

In the United States, the two major parties act as if they hate each other. In campaigning, the message is not, "I will do better for you than my opponent will." That would be a positive politics, and that's fair. If you're being positive, you can say, "look, my opponent can't deliver what I can deliver for you." It's a valid comparison and positive in its net result. But politics today is the antagonistic politics of "we need to save our country from the other side. The other candidate wants to destroy America!" It's not just one party doing this. Both parties are doing this.

When electoral politics is dominated, even strangled, by this rhetoric of "apocalypse averted if you vote for me, apocalypse assured if you vote for him or her," that's the extreme version of antagonistic politics. That's the form of politics long practiced by American nationalists, including the MAGA movement, and now of much of the Democratic Party that feels it needs to match antagonism with antagonism.

Agonistic Politics

Another form is agonistic politics. "Agonistic" is an odd word in this context because we think about agony as painful and brutal (though sometimes politics can be). But in philosophical concepts, to say that something is agonistic refers to the idea that there are conflicts of opinions and struggles for power. We see this in elections when multiple candidates try to convince citizens to vote for them. We also see it in legislative governance when politicians debate legislation.

Chantal Mouffe defines the difference between antagonistic and agonistic forms of politics as the difference between the categories of enemy and adversary:

> This means that within the "we" that constitutes the political community, the opponent is not considered an enemy to be destroyed but an adversary whose existence is legitimate. His ideas will be fought with vigour but his right to defend them will never be questioned. The category of enemy does not disappear, however, for it remains pertinent with regard to those who, by questioning the very principles of pluralist democracy, cannot form part of the agonistic space.[146]

We can disagree without seeing politics as a holy crusade requiring a scorched-earth policy. The British Parliament long referred to minority parties as "the loyal opposition"—loyal to the country but in opposition to the majority party currently in power. This value of combining loyalty with principled disagreement is essential to a peaceful, functioning democratic government.[147]

Deliberative Politics

The third form of politics is deliberative politics. This is first and foremost the idea that we could have a different politics if we choose to build one—a nonantagonistic, nonagonistic politics, one that practices deliberation among people and looks for cooperation and solidarity more than it looks for conflict.

Deliberative politics seeks common action and common benefit. There are ideal and nonideal versions of this form of

---

[146] Chantal Mouffe, "Agonistic Democracy and Radical Politics," *Pavillion Journal of Politics and Culture*, December 29, 2014, https://www.pavilionmagazine.org/chantal-mouffe-agonistic-democracy-and-radical-politics/.

[147] George Anastaplo, "Loyal Opposition in a Modern Democracy," *Loyola University Chicago Law Journal*, Volume 35, Issue 4, Summer 2004, https://core.ac.uk/download/pdf/268429712.pdf.

politics. John Rawls's version is the most well-known version; his ideal theory is based on his definition that justice is fairness. Rawls contends that if we step back and objectively and rationally consider the ideal type of society we want, we will then be able to come to a consensus on how we want society to be, and then we could act to make society in that image.[148] Such a view is overly idealistic, neglecting both the social realities of historical inequalities among people and the reality that people have rational but incompatible visions of how a fair and just society would be structured.

A nonideal form of deliberative politics takes into account that consensus is not easy to achieve, and that political debate will seldom reach the closure of ideal solutions. The most well-known theory of a deliberative society has been put forth by Amy Gutmann and Dennis Thompson. They label it "deliberative democracy," which has the ethical value that "persons should be treated not merely as objects of legislation, as passive subjects to be ruled, but as autonomous agents who take part in the governance of their own society, directly or through their representatives."[149]

In deliberative democracy, people are empowered to contribute to political decision-making but must abide by legislative decisions that are properly made. The requirement to obey the law implies a form of closure but not of finality. Governmental decisions must be justified, open to deliberation and discussion, and open to change when necessary. In other words, citizens should be allowed fair and equal access to the process of making laws but should respect and follow laws fairly created and enforced while still retaining the right to call into question problems with laws. The obligation of government is to establish processes of political deliberation and ensure that they are transparent and

---

[148] John Rawls, *A Theory of Justice* (Belknap Press, 1971).
[149] Amy Gutmann and Dennis Thompson, *Why Deliberative Democracy?* (Princeton University Press, 2004).

openly accessible by all. Deliberative politics is a dynamic, continual process.

Any form of fair and transparent deliberative democracy would require effort and patience. People prone to lazy thinking would probably find it too lengthy and laborious. The values of inclusion and equal access to power would be unacceptable to reactionaries and others who seek greater power concentrations. Such resistance does not negate the ideas, values, and potential benefits of deliberative democracy. Such objections illustrate the need for fairer and more accessible political processes that circulate power to more people.

The problem is that there are people and movements who actively oppose moves to bring more people into political processes. Some of these people claim to love America and want to make it great but don't want to apply the American values of liberty and justice for all.

Recognizing Reality and Each Other

Reality is complex, and no part of reality is more complex than human society. Why politics is currently so toxic is definitely a result of many complex factors. One of those factors is the issue of recognition versus misrecognition, and recognition theory holds the key to understanding so much of human society and so much of human behavior. A brief discussion of the concept of recognition will help explain antagonism in politics.

For centuries, some philosophers have discussed the importance of recognition.[150] Recognition theory gives us a way to more easily understand social norms and behaviors. Recognition, simply put, is the idea that I see you and I recognize that you are a person, and as such, you deserve to be

---

[150] Axel Honneth, *Recognition: A Chapter in the History of European Ideas* (Cambridge University Press, 2021).

treated in certain ways. If you are a person, you have rights and certain privileges. If you are a person, I have certain ethical obligations to you and to act accordingly to you.

Recognition norms are ways in which a society instructs people, either implicitly or explicitly, on what to value, how to behave, and how to react when seeing these values and traits in other people. If someone is behaving properly, we are taught to recognize them and treat them in ways a worthy person deserves to be treated. If someone is not behaving according to recognition norms defining how a person should act in our society, then we are entitled, if not obligated, to treat them quite differently.

One example of recognition norms is how society says we should treat someone who has committed a crime. They are still human beings. They still have rights, but if they've committed a crime, they have violated recognition norms and therefore they have lost a certain right to certain treatments. We punish them. We may put them in jail or prison. They lose some, but not all, of their rights; they may lose some of their property, or they may be required to make restitution because they violated our society's recognition norms. It's most easily seen in criminal conduct, but we see this in all areas and aspects of human society. Someone who is just rude, someone who just doesn't play along well with others, is also treated with appropriate disapproval.

The current state of politics in the United States is marked by fault lines defined by differing recognition norms. How recognition has manifested in politics is that recognition norms have been linked to holding certain positions or simply membership in a political party. People holding divergent political positions and the opposition parties themselves are judged as having transgressed norms of proper thought and behavior, actions that call for disapproval and even condemnation akin to them having committed criminal acts. Political opponents are denied recognition—they are misrecognized—and considered unworthy of full inclusion within ethical consideration.

Misrecognizing and condemning people who have different political opinions is the norm for American nationalism and its current incarnation as the MAGA movement. People who are American nationalists see their reactionary political opinions as normative values akin to moral values, and they treat all who disagree with their opinions as enemies instead of adversaries. Theirs is an antagonistic politics in which the opposition is composed of enemies who must be destroyed, and compromise or even dialogue with them is immoral.

Conspiracy theories are part and parcel of antagonistic politics. The more a society gives in to antagonism and demonizing the other side, the more it opens the door to dualistic apocalyptic thinking of an ultimate battle of good and evil. If you think that people different from you are evil, you tend not to be satisfied with just simply hating them for tangible reasons. You will create new reasons to hate them. And this cycle perpetuates conspiracy theories and manifests ultimately in violent acts.

The MAGA movement is not alone in such antagonistic behavior. On the other side of this dualism of MAGA's recognition norms are those who oppose Trump and the people who support him; they are enemies who must be destroyed.

Self-defense against those seeking to destroy you is sensible and laudable, but one has to ask if answering antagonistic politics with equivalent antagonism is at all helpful. Doesn't mutual hating and despising just perpetuate a cycle of antagonism that prevents any positive outcomes? That's what we have now in the petty feud between the reactionary Right and the fake Left.[151]

---

[151] Giles, *Left Wing, Right Wing*, 79–85.

To understand antagonistic politics, and the alternative, Mouffe's distinction between the categories of enemy and adversary is useful when combined with the concept of recognition. To view someone as an enemy is to remove that person from recognition and ethical consideration. Calvinism's dualistic worldview of good and evil, Elect and damned, is an example—a worldview that became ingrained in American culture. It is an attitude that creates the conditions for abuses of other people because to misrecognize (deny) their human rights and even their humanity is ethically required by the dualistic recognition norms. For example, in reactionism's dualism, calling immigrants "vermin" becomes ethically good behavior and should be applauded. Condemning immigrants and anyone friendly to them as corruption that needs to be "drained" away or destroyed becomes a sign of moral purity.

What's the alternative? Recognizing the humanity of others. Everyone. That means recognizing our opponents as adversaries rather than as enemies and being willing to oppose the injustices inflicted by those who see others as enemies. It's a tricky balance of meaningful opposition without descending into antagonism, but a better society is possible if we can achieve that balance.

This doesn't mean rolling over and not opposing injustice and those who inflict injustices on others. Just as we can disagree without being disagreeable, we can oppose evil without becoming evil, if "evil" is even the proper term. Where there are disputes, we can defend what we see as the good without declaring our adversaries to be criminals, evil, and enemies to be destroyed.

We can firmly say, "my opponent does not agree with me on issues A, B, and C, and I believe that their disagreement on issues A, B, and C is harmful to the social welfare of our country." That's perfectly legitimate. It's a bit of a journey, but not too long of a journey to go from that very civil—still agonistic but very civil—disagreement to, "my opponent does not agree with A, B, and C; therefore, my opponent is an enemy of the people, an enemy of the state, and a danger to our society and needs to be purged from government! Vote for me!"

Or it's not at all "vote for me." It's "be sure to vote AGAINST my evil and corrupt opponent!" And I'm not really exaggerating some of the rhetoric that's going on in electoral races today. The primary message of politics today is an exhortation to actively misrecognize other people who have different views. The dominant antagonisms across US politicians and their surrogates are active attempts to prevent dialogue about issues and deny others' access to political processes.

Eyes-Wide-Open Politics

Antagonistic politics is an end of dialogue, an attempt to silence the other side, to silence viewpoints different from your own. It is a form of cowardice—a refusal to be courageous enough to acknowledge that other people have a right to their opinions. Agonistic politics is a step better in acknowledging that there will be conflict in politics but not letting political differences descend into antagonism.

Deliberative politics steps further away from antagonism by recognizing the value of open political processes and greater circulation of power. Deliberative politics also doesn't settle, as agonistic politics can, for permanent division and conflict. For example, Mouffe, whose views are informed by neo-Marxism, rejects deliberative politics because she believes that division and antagonism cannot be eradicated. She believes that every social order is about domination, public life being defined by collective identities of "we" and "they" with no possibility whatsoever of final reconciliation.[152]

---

[152] Mouffe,"Agonistic Democracy."

We need not resign ourselves to permanent division, as Mouffe does. However, it is too simplistic to just say, "let's just stop being antagonistic towards each other, let's stop thinking that our system needs to be agonistic." Society is complex, so disagreements among people will be a fundamental part of society. People will have disputes, and they need to resolve those disputes. It would be far better if they resolved disputes with recognition constantly in mind.

The reality is that to disagree with someone does not mean that person is evil, bad, and stupid. It just means they disagree with you. Even when they are factually incorrect, they aren't necessarily evil. It takes a certain amount of courage, a certain amount of maturity, to accept that other people disagree with you. It's okay. Intelligent minds can disagree. Sincere people can disagree and can be incorrect.

That said, I am in no way Pollyannaish in believing that every disagreement is just a matter of intelligent disagreement between sincere individuals. There are certain beliefs and certain attitudes that are reprehensible, fundamentally reprehensible, and have no place within a just society. Much of the history discussed in this book describes such attitudes.

That's where recognition norms apply. You can have a sincere respectful, civil, but firm disagreement, or you can just be antagonistic and dangerous. Yes, we do need to stand up against injustice and ressentiment-fueled bigotry. I'm not denying that there are abhorrent attitudes and people doing abhorrent things. A bromide of "we'll just work for consensus, we'll just cooperate with each other, we'll find solidarity" won't work in the face of reactionary ressentiment. We have to disagree and disagree as strongly as is necessary but no stronger.

Recognition itself is an agonistic process. It's not immediate, it's not simple, it's not easy at times, but it is necessary. If that's preachy, fine, that's preachy. Recognize other people as human beings, even when they're behaving unlike human beings, even when they're engaging in antagonistic politics and condemning you as the devil incarnate. You're not, and they know you're not. So just call their bluff on it.

Responding to Trump and the MAGA Movement

What about Trump? How should we respond to his lies and conspiracy theories? Should Trump be deplatformed, silenced, or censored? Are Trump's corruption and bigotry enough of a problem to warrant silencing him? That's the question, and it is a profound one. That is because it isn't so much about Trump as it is about the larger question of the effects of harmful speech and what a positive response to it is.

If you want to deplatform Trump because you don't like him or don't like what he says, that is not sufficient reason to silence him or anyone else. The same is true if you disagree with Trump's (or anyone else's) policies. There are better, more mature, responses.

Early in my academic career, I was on a panel discussing free speech. Preserving academic freedom has long been a concern of mine. During my turn to speak, I gave a fairly pedestrian answer about the importance of recognizing free speech. The professor who came after me started his comments with the statement:

All speech should be permitted except speech that seeks to silence other people.

That remains one of the most profoundly wise ideas I have heard. It is a principle I have tried to apply ever since.

I combine that principle with John Stuart Mill's idea that the answer to wrong speech is more speech.[153] If someone is telling untruths, the constructive reply is to speak the truth. If you can't answer what you believe are errors by detailing the truth, then you need to reassess your position or better prepare your facts in response.

---

[153] John Stuart Mill, *On Liberty* (Hackett Publishing, 1978).

What Mill did not adequately consider are situations in which one is not allowed to respond to wrong speech with the truth. In the century and a half since Mill's time, philosophy and the world in general have become far more aware of the realities that many people are denied the opportunity to participate in social institutions and social discourse. Simply saying that people should speak up in response to untruths ignores underlying issues of injustice and inequality that prevent people from being heard.

That is a big reason why I find value in the principle that speech should be permitted except speech that seeks to silence other people. It shifts the subject from "do we like this speech?" to "does this speech harm other people?" Getting to that question was much of Mill's motivation with his concept of the harm principle. Speech and actions should not be restricted unless they cause harm to others. Speech that silences other people is harming them, so according to the harm principle, we are permitted and even have a duty to restrict such speech.

I interpret the question of whether one is silencing others more broadly than silencing speech acts. Preventing someone from participating in society, such as the legal system, fair employment, and so on, is effectively silencing that person. Calling for others to condemn and harass a group of people is an attempt to silence those people.

We have no right to prevent other people from having and expressing their opinions and ideas. That's why the right to free expression is enshrined in law. However, no rights are infinite, and no freedom comes without an equal or greater amount of responsibility. You have no right to harm others, so if you use your freedom to harm others, you deserve to lose the freedom that you abused.

Hate speech and conspiracy theories that defame and call for hostility toward a group of people are attempts to silence those people. Those who engage in attempts to silence others have abused their freedom. They deserve to lose the freedom to engage in such actions.

The devil is in the details, of course, and in the nuances of speech acts. It is simple to say that someone trying to incite a riot or saying that people in Group X should be abused or killed are attempts to silence others and that that person has lost the right to say such things. But what about the myriad forms of propaganda, dog whistles, and leading innuendos that are spoken? It is difficult to know where to draw the line.

That's where we can return to Mill's ideas. We need to answer speech that harms others but that doesn't permit us to silence others. Our first instinct should not be to deplatform others by shutting them down or shouting them down. Simplistic answers are tempting but almost always wrong. Censoring speech is often counterproductive. We need to be careful even if we feel our justification is sound.

Should Trump be given a national platform, or should he be prevented from speaking? Well, why are you asking? That may say more about you than about him. If you have a good argument that Trump is seeking to silence people, then give it. More speech is the answer to wrong speech, and the only legitimate reason to restrict speech is when it is trying to silence others.

That said, there are good arguments that Trump and people who support him are trying to silence others. Trump campaigns not with policies but with emotions. He doesn't give positive solutions but engages in the dualism that all with whom he disagrees are his enemies. In the call and response between Trump and the MAGA movement, Trump gives the reactionaries the ressentiment they want to hear, and they eagerly repeat it—defaming and calling for hostility toward other people.

But again, there's little new in what Trump says. He's a loud, angry focal point for the old reactionary strain of American politics. Yes, Trump lies, and so do those in the MAGA movement and the larger American nationalist subculture, but we need to deal with causes, not symptoms. Making them enemies and shouting back accomplishes nothing. Until we respond to the reactionary ressentiment by talking openly and firmly about what's behind their angry demands and lies, the cycle will just continue.

Actually, responding to the MAGA movement with antagonism let's them silence us. Because then we are letting them be the center of attention when the discussion should be how we can address the problems we face and what solutions we can craft to deal with those problems.

And yes, American nationalism and all of its antagonism are problems that we face. But our discussion should be about the causes of their attitudes and antagonism and how to mitigate those causes and the harms they inflict on people.

We need to talk about ressentiment and the fearful reactions to difference. We need to talk about lazy thinking and conspiracy theories. These realities are found in people from across the political spectrum.

We need to talk about jingoism and the influence of Calvinism. We need to talk about the United States' long history of anti-immigrant rhetoric and the harms it has caused to the country. We need to be honest about what bigotry is and how it fuels American nationalism and spurs the victimhood claims of the reactionary Right.

We can't hope to stop the cycle of hate and ignorance created by the weaknesses of ressentiment and the false moral judgments those feelings create until we talk about them. We also need to not fight *against* something as much as fight *for* something.

I don't offer a simple solution because there is none. But it does have to begin with recognition and continue on to dialogue and fighting *for* positive, constructive values. It does have to begin with recognition of other human beings as human beings, recognizing other individuals as individuals.

Then the real work begins.

Reference List

America Library Association. "Book Ban Data: Banned and Challenged Books." Accessed June 22, 2024. https://www.ala.org/bbooks/book-ban-data.

Anastaplo, George. "Loyal Opposition in a Modern Democracy." *Loyola University Chicago Law Journal*, Volume 35, Issue 4, Summer 2004. https://core.ac.uk/download/pdf/268429712.pdf.

Anbinder, Tyler. "The Long, Ugly History Of Insisting Minority Groups Can't Criticize America." *The Washington Post*, July 19, 2019. https://www.washingtonpost.com/outlook/2019/07/19/long-ugly-history-insisting-minority-groups-cant-criticize-america/.

Anthony, Ted. "Love him? Hate him? For Donald Trump, Attention is Attention." *Associated Press,* April 4, 2023. https://apnews.com/article/trump-attention-indictment-arraignment-president-1e87be51004b12dc7b85728fd7946b56.

Asia Pacific Curriculum. "Chinese Migrations in the Mid-Late 19th Century." Accessed June 21,2024. https://asiapacificcurriculum.ca/learning-module/chinese-migrations-mid-late-19th-century.

Baird, Andrew F., J. Micah Roos, and J. Scott Carter. "Understanding the Rise of Anti-Political Correctness Sentiment: The Curious Role of Education." *Humanity & Society*, Volume 47, Issue 1, September 1, 2021. https://journals.sagepub.com/doi/full/10.1177/01605976221120536#bibr27-01605976221120536.

Barkun, Michael. "Conspiracy Theories about Barack Obama." In *A Culture of Conspiracy*. University of California Press, 2013.

Barlow, Rich. "Are Trump Republicans Fascists?" *BU Today*, February 11, 2022. https://www.bu.edu/articles/2022/are-trump-republicans-fascists/.

Barth, F. Diane. "How Can We Understand Our Fear of the Other?" *Psychology Today*, March 11, 2016. https://www.psychologytoday.com/us/blog/the-couch/201603/how-can-we-understand-our-fear-the-other.

Bates, Suzanne. "Poll: Republicans see Trump as a 'Person of Faith' ... More so than Mitt Romney, Mike Pence and Others." *Deseret News*, September 26, 2023. https://www.deseret.com/2023/9/26/23891360/trump-biden-man-of-faith-religious-mitt-romney-vivek-ramaswamy/.

Bellah, Robert Neelly. "Civil Religion in America." *Dædalus, Journal of the American Academy of Arts and Sciences* 96 (1), 1967: 1–21.

Bender, Michael C. "The Church of Trump: How He's Infusing Christianity Into His Movement." *New York Times*, April 1, 2024, https://www.nytimes.com/2024/04/01/us/politics/trump-2024-religion.html.

Bercovitch, Sacvan. *The Puritan Origins of the American Self.* Yale University Press, 1975.

Blackburn, Marsha. "Why Is Critical Race Theory Dangerous For Our Kids?" July 21, 2021. https://www.blackburn.senate.gov/2021/7/why-is-critical-race-theory-dangerous-for-our-kids.

Bloom, Harold. *Jesus and Yahweh: The Names Divine.* Riverhead, 2005.

Blumenthal, Sidney. "Trump's Legal Woes Are Part of His Quasi-religious Mythology of Martyrdom." *The Guardian*, August 21, 2024. https://www.theguardian.com/commentisfree/2023/aug/21/trump-election-giuliani-sidney-blumenthal.

Boissoneault, Lorraine. "How the 19th-Century Know Nothing Party Reshaped American Politics." *Smithsonian Magazine*, January 26. 2017. https://www.smithsonianmag.com/history/immigrants-conspiracies-and-secret-society-launched-american-nativism-180961915/.

Bolton, Alexander. "Former Speaker Ryan: 'Trump's Not a Conservative, He's an Authoritarian Narcissist.'" *The Hill*, December 12, 2023. https://thehill.com/homenews/house/4359176-former-speaker-ryan-trumps-not-a-conservative-hes-an-authoritarian-narcissist/.

Britannica, T. Editors of Encyclopaedia. "Protocols of the Elders of Zion." *Encyclopedia Britannica*, May 29, 2024. https://www.britannica.com/topic/Protocols-of-the-Elders-of-Zion.

Britannica, The Editors of Encyclopaedia. "Michael Servetus." *Encyclopedia Britannica*, April 8, 2024. https://www.britannica.com/biography/Michael-Servetus.

Bruder, Emily. "When 20,000 American Nazis Descended Upon New York City." *The Atlantic*, October 10, 2017. https://www.theatlantic.com/video/index/542499/marshall-curry-nazi-rally-madison-square-garden-1939/.

Bump, Philip. "Democrats and Republicans are Equally Likely to Say the Other Party's Candidate Is 'Too Corrupt.'" *The Washington Post*, March 15, 2024. https://www.washingtonpost.com/politics/2024/03/15/biden-trump-corrupt-poll/.

Burke, Daniel. "The Guilt-free Gospel of Donald Trump." *CNN*, October 24, 2016. https://www.cnn.com/2016/10/21/politics/trump-religion-gospel/index.html.

Butler University Information Commons. "Banned Books: Reasons Books are Challenged." Accessed June 22, 2024. https://libguides.butler.edu/bannedbooks?p=217686.

Calvin, John. *Institutes of the Christian Religion*. Translated by Henry Beveridge. Hendrickson Publishers, 2008.

Cambridge English Dictionary. "Wokeness." Accessed June 25, 2024. https://dictionary.cambridge.org/us/dictionary/english/wokeness.

Campbell, Bradley and Jason Manning. *The Rise of Victimhood Culture: Microaggressions, Safe Spaces, and the New Culture Wars*. Palgrave Macmillan, 2018.

Carpiano, Richard M., Timothy Callaghan, Renee DiResta, Noel T. Brewer, Chelsea Clinton, Alison P. Galvani, et. al. "Confronting the Evolution and Expansion of Anti-vaccine Activism in the USA in the COVID-19 Era." *Lancet*. 2023;401(10380):967-970.

Carstairs, Catherine. "Debating Water Fluoridation Before Dr. Strangelove." *American Journal of Public Health*, Aug;105(8), 2016, 1559-69.

Cashman, Sean Dennis. *America in the Gilded Age, Third Edition*. New York University Press, 1993.

The Constitution of the United States: A Transcription." *National Archives and Records Administration*. November 4, 2015, https://www.archives.gov/founding-docs/constitution-transcript.

Conway, Kellyanne. "Meet the Press" interview broadcast January 22, 2017. https://www.nbcnews.com/meet-the-press/video/conway-press-secretary-gave-alternative-facts-860142147643.

Council on Foreign Relations. "Excerpt: Isolationism—An Anatomy of Isolationism." Accessed June 7, 2024. https://www.cfr.org/excerpt-isolationism,

The Daily Show. "June 3, 2024 – Rep. Ken Buck." https://www.cc.com/episodes/bse7mc/the-daily-show-june-3-2024-rep-ken-buck-season-29-ep-53.

Dallek, Matthew. "The GOP Has a Long History of Ignoring Science. Trump Turned It into Policy." *The Washington Post,* October 9, 2020. https://www.washingtonpost.com/outlook/the-gop-has-a-long-history-of-ignoring-science-trump-turned-it-into-policy/2020/10/09/53574602-0917-11eb-859b-f9c27abe638d_story.html.

Danielson, Leilah. "Civil Religion as Myth, Not History." *Religions* (2019) *10*(6): 374. https://www.mdpi.com/2077-1444/10/6/374.

von Däniken, Erich. *Chariots of the Gods?* Putnam, 1969.

Dawsey, Josh, Rosalind S. Helderman, and David A. Fahrenthold. "How Trump Abandoned His Pledge To 'Drain The Swamp.'" *Washington Post,* October 24, 2020. https://www.washingtonpost.com/politics/trump-drain-the-swamp/2020/10/24/52c7682c-0a5a-11eb-9be6-cf25fb429f1a_story.html.

Debenedetti, Gabriel. "They Always Wanted Trump." *Politico Magazine,* November 07,2016. https://www.politico.com/magazine/story/2016/11/hillary-clinton-2016-donald-trump-214428/.

Descartes, René. *Discourse on the Method of Rightly Conducting One's Reason and of Seeking Truth.* Project Gutenberg. Accessed June 17, 2024. http://www.gutenberg.org/ebooks/59.

Diamond, Jeremy. "Donald Trump: Ban all Muslim Travel to U.S." *CNN,* December 7, 2015. https://www.cnn.com/2015/12/07/politics/donald-trump-muslim-ban-immigration/index.html.

Diaz, Jaclyn. "The Charges Facing Trump in the Jan. 6 Investigation, Explained." *NPR,* August 2, 2023. https://www.npr.org/2023/08/01/1191493880/trump-january-6-charges-indictment-counts.

Dickson, E. J. "Former QAnon Followers Explain What Drew Them In—And Got Them Out." *Rolling Stone,* September 23, 2020. https://www.rollingstone.com/culture/culture-features/ex-qanon-followers-cult-conspiracy-theory-pizzagate-1064076/.

DiPrete, Thomas A., Andrew Gelman, Tyler McCormick, Julian Teitler, and Tian Zheng. "Segregation in Social Networks Based on Acquaintanceship and Trust." *American Journal of Sociology* Vol. 116, No. 4 (January 2011): 1234-83.

Downen, Robert. "At Texas GOP Convention, Republicans Call for Spiritual Warfare." *The Texas Tribune*, May 28, 2024. https://www.texastribune.org/2024/05/28/texas-gop-convention-elections-religion-delegates-platform/.

Dwyer, Colin. "Donald Trump: 'I Could ... Shoot Somebody, and I Wouldn't Lose Any Voters.'" NPR, January 23, 2016. https://www.npr.org/sections/thetwo-way/2016/01/23/464129029/donald-trump-i-could-shoot-somebody-and-i-wouldnt-lose-any-voters.

The Economist. "Scientists Dispute a Suggestion that SARS-CoV-2 Was Engineered." *The Economist*, October 27, 2022. https://www.economist.com/science-and-technology/2022/10/27/scientists-dispute-a-suggestion-that-sars-cov-2-was-engineered.

Ecosia powered by Oxford Languages. "Wokeness." Accessed June 25, 2024. https://www.ecosia.org/search?q=wokeness.

Eddy, Bill. "Malignant Narcissism: Does the President Really Have It?" *High Conflict Institute*, March 19,2019. https://highconflictinstitute.com/personality-disorders/malignant-narcissism-does-the-president-really-have-it/.

Everett. "Anti-Irish Song. No Irish Need Apply." *FineArtAmerica*. Accessed June 29, 2024. https://fineartamerica.com/featured/anti-irish-song-no-irish-need-apply-everett.html?product=poster.

Feuerherd, Peter. "John Calvin: The Religious Reformer Who Influenced Capitalism." *JSTOR Daily*, July 10, 2017. https://daily.jstor.org/john-calvin-religious-reformer-influenced-capitalism/.

France 24. "Trump Turns New York Fraud Trial into Campaign Stop, 'A Witch Hunt.'" March 10, 2023. https://www.france24.com/en/americas/20231003-trump-turns-new-york-fraud-trial-into-campaign-stop-a-witch-hunt.

Garcia, Eric. "A History of 'Draining the Swamp." *Roll Call*, October 18, 2016. https://rollcall.com/2016/10/18/a-history-of-draining-the-swamp/.

Geisst, Charles R. *Wall Street: A History*. Oxford University Press, 1999.

George W. Bush Presidential Library. "Global War on Terror." Accessed July 11, 2024. https://www.georgewbushlibrary.gov/research/topic-guides/global-war-terror.

Giles, Douglas. *Left Wing, Right Wing, People, and Power: The Core Dynamics of Political Action*. Real Clear Philosophy, 2024.

Giles, Douglas. *Rethinking Misrecognition and Struggles for Recognition*. Insert Philosophy, 2020.

Goldenberg, David M. *The Curse of Ham: Race and Slavery in Early Judaism, Christianity, and Islam*. Princeton University Press, 2003.

Grad, Shelby. "The Racist Massacre that Killed 10% of L.A.'s Chinese Population and Brought Shame to the City." *Los Angeles Times*, March 18, 2021. https://www.latimes.com/california/story/2021-03-18/reflecting-los-angeles-chinatown-massacre-after-atlanta-shootings.

Gutmann, Amy, and Dennis Thompson. *Why Deliberative Democracy?* Princeton University Press, 2004.

Han, Hyemin. "Debunking Trump's Witch Hunt Theory." *Lawfare*, June 16, 2023. https://www.lawfaremedia.org/article/debunking-trump-s-witch-hunt-theory.

Hansen, Liane, and David Folkenflik. "The Power of the 24-Hour News Cycle." *NPR*, May 29, 2005. https://www.npr.org/2005/05/29/4671485/the-power-of-the-24-hour-news-cycle.

Hawthorne, Nathaniel. *The Scarlet Letter*. Penguin, 2015.

Heritage Action for America. "Reject Critical Race Theory." Accessed June 25, 2024. https://heritageaction.com/toolkit/rejectcrt.

Honneth, Axel. *Recognition: A Chapter in the History of European Ideas*. Cambridge University Press, 2021.

Hutson, Matthew. "A Conspiracy of Loneliness." *Scientific American Mind*, Vol. 28 No. 3. May 2017, 15.

Jackson Sow, Marissa. "Whiteness as Guilt: Attacking Critical Race Theory to Redeem the Racial Contract." *UCLA Law Review*, March 29, 2022. https://www.uclalawreview.org/whiteness-as-guilt-attacking-critical-race-theory-to-redeem-the-racial-contract/.

James, Frank. "Sen. Mitch McConnell Insists: One and Done for Obama." *It's All Politics: NPR*, November 4, 2020. https://www.npr.org/sections/itsallpolitics/2010/11/04/131069048/sen-mcconnell-insists-one-term-for-obama.

James, William. *The Meaning of Truth*. Flame Tree 451, 2024.

Jameson, Frederic. *The Political Unconscious: Narrative as a Socially Symbolic Act*. Cornell University Press, 1981.

Jesus (attributed). Gospel of Matthew 5:14, *King James Version*.

Johnson, Carina L. "Mobilizing Fear: Propagandizing German–Ottoman Conflict." *The American Academy in Berlin*. Accessed June 26, 2024. https://www.americanacademy.de/mobilizing-fear/.

Kahneman, Daniel. *Thinking, Fast and Slow*. Farrar, Straus, and Giroux, 2011.

Kapur, Sahlil. "Trump Revives Old Battle Cry Against 2020 Democrats: Socialism." *Bloomberg*, March 7, 2019. https://www.bloomberg.com/news/articles/2019-03-07/trump-revives-old-battle-cry-against-2020-democrats-socialism.

Kim, Soo Rin. "Trump Associates Who Have Been Sent to Prison or Faced Criminal Charges." *ABC News*, January 17, 2020. https://abcnews.go.com/Politics/trump-associates-prison-faced-criminal-charges/story?id=68358219.

Kluger, Jeffrey. "The Truth about Donald Trump's Narcissism." *Time*, August 11, 2015. https://time.com/3992363/trump-narcissism/.

Kohut, Andrew, and Bruce Stokes. "The Problem of American Exceptionalism." *Pew Research Center*, May 9, 2006. https://www.pewresearch.org/politics/2006/05/09/the-problem-of-american-exceptionalism/.

Lamont, Michèle, Bo Yun Park, and Elena Ayala-Hurtado. "Trump's Electoral Speeches and His Appeal to the American White Working Class." *The British Journal of Sociology* 68(S1):S153–S180, 2017.

Langewiesche, William. "Vanished: How Malaysia Airlines Flight 370 Disappeared." *The Atlantic*, June 17, 2019. https://medium.com/the-atlantic/vanished-how-malaysia-airlines-flight-370-disappeared-ecc0afa78335.

Lehmann, Chris. "The Self-Help Guru Who Shaped Trump's Worldview." *In These Times*, December 13, 2017. https://inthesetimes.com/article/Trump-White-House-Self-Help-Norman-Vincent-Peale-MAGA.

Leingang, Rachel. "'No Way Out without Bloodshed': The Right Believe the US Is under Threat and Are Mobilizing." *The Guardian*, June 2, 2024. https://www.theguardian.com/us-news/article/2024/jun/02/far-right-mobilizing-biden-presidency.

LeVine, Marianne and Meryl Kornfield, "Trump's Anti-immigrant Onslaught Sparks Fresh Alarm Heading into 2024." *The Washington Post*, October 12, 2023. https://www.washingtonpost.com/elections/2023/10/12/trump-immigrants-comments-criticism/.

Library of Congress. "William McKinley Assassination: Topics in Chronicling America." Accessed June 30, 2024. https://guides.loc.gov/chronicling-america-william-mckinley-assassination.

Matthews, Jr., Robert E. "Button, Ronald Reagan, 1980." The Smithsonian Institution. Accessed June 7, 2024, https://www.si.edu/object/button-ronald-reagan-1980%3Anmah_522618.

McCormick, Charles H. *Hopeless Cases: The Hunt for the Red Scare Terrorist Bombers*. University Press of America, 2005.

McGrath, Alister E. *A Life of John Calvin: A Study in the Shaping of Western Culture*. Wiley-Blackwell, 1993.

McKenna, George. *The Puritan Origins of American Patriotism*, Yale University Press, 2009.

Merriam-Webster. "Chauvinism." *Merriam-Webster.com Dictionary*, s.v. Accessed June 20, 2024. https://www.merriam-webster.com/dictionary/chauvinism.

Merriam-Webster. "Jingoism." *Merriam-Webster.com Dictionary*, s.v. Accessed June 20, 2024. https://www.merriam-webster.com/dictionary/jingoism,

Merriam-Webster. "Patriotism." *Merriam-Webster.com Dictionary*, s.v. Accessed June 20, 2024. https://www.merriam-webster.com/dictionary/patriotism.

Merriam-Webster. "Ressentiment." *Merriam-Webster.com Dictionary*, s.v. Accessed 16 June 2024. https://www.merriam-webster.com/dictionary/ressentiment.

Merriam-Webster. "Sheeple." *Merriam-Webster.com Dictionary*, s.v. Accessed June 19, 2024. https://www.merriam-webster.com/dictionary/sheeple.

Mill, John Stuart. *On Liberty*. Hackett Publishing, 1978.

Miller, Arthur. *The Crucible: A Play in Four Acts*. Penguin, 2003.

Mills, Charles W. *The Racial Contract*. Cornell University Press, 1997.

Mills, David. "The Dangerous Christian Belief that Donald Trump Is a 'Man of Faith.'" *Pittsburgh Post-Gazette*, June 22, 2024. https://www.post-gazette.com/opinion/david-mills/2024/01/08/david-mills-evangelicalism-trump-christianity/stories/202401080097.

Mouffe, Chantal. "Agonistic Democracy and Radical Politics." *Pavillion Journal of Politics and Culture.* December 29, 2014. https://www.pavilionmagazine.org/chantal-mouffe-agonistic-democracy-and-radical-politics/.

Murray, Douglas, and Lex Fridman. "War on White People." June 22, 2022. https://www.youtube.com/watch?v=FJlRJ-1kgqw.

NAACP. "Reclaiming the Word "Woke" as Part of African American Culture." 2023. https://naacp.org/resources/reclaiming-word-woke-part-african-american-culture.

National Archives. "Japanese-American Incarceration During World War II." Last reviewed on March 22, 2024. https://www.archives.gov/education/lessons/japanese-relocation.

The New York Times. "The Gingrich Coup." November 7, 1998. https://www.nytimes.com/1998/11/07/opinion/the-gingrich-coup.html.

Newsweek, "Donald Trump Admits He's Not a Conservative." March 11, 2024. https://www.newsweek.com/donald-trump-admits-he-isnt-conservative-cnbc-squawk-box-1877949.

Nietzsche, Friedrich. *On the Genealogy of Morals.* Edited by Kieth Ansell-Pearson. Translated by Carol Diethe. Cambridge University Press, 2007.

Nozick, Robert. *Anarchy, State, and Utopia.* Blackwell, 1974.

Office of the Historian, US State Department. "The Immigration Act of 1924 (The Johnson-Reed Act)." Accessed June 30, 2024, https://history.state.gov/milestones/1921-1936/immigration-act.

Page, Clarence. "Why Donald Trump Appeals to Disaffected White Voters." *Chicago Tribune*, Nov 10, 2015. https://www.chicagotribune.com/2015/11/10/why-donald-trump-appeals-to-disaffected-white-voters/.

PBS News. "One Year Ago, Republicans Condemned Jan. 6 Insurrection. Yesterday, Their Response Was Far More Muted." January 7, 2022. https://www.pbs.org/newshour/politics/one-year-ago-republicans-condemned-jan-6-insurrection-yesterday-their-response-was-far-more-muted.

PBS News. "WATCH LIVE: Trump attends presidential campaign rally in Racine, Wisconsin." June 18.2024. https://www.youtube.com/watch?v=X-XYXZXh-Hc.

Plato. *Republic*. Project Gutenberg. Accessed June 17, 2024. http://www.gutenberg.org/ebooks/1497.

Press, Bill. *The Obama Hate Machine: The Lies, Distortions, and Personal Attacks on the President---and Who Is Behind Them*. Thomas Dunne Books, 2012.

Rawls, John. *A Theory of Justice*. Belknap Press, 1971.

Reeve, W. Paul. *Religion of a Different Color: Race and the Mormon Struggle for Whiteness*. Oxford University Press, 2015.

Reuters. "What Trump Allies Have Faced Criminal Charges?" August 2, 2023. https://www.reuters.com/world/us/many-trumps-orbit-have-faced-criminal-charges-2023-02-16/.

Roose, Kevin. "What Is QAnon, the Viral Pro-Trump Conspiracy Theory?" *New York Times*, Sep 3, 2021. https://www.nytimes.com/article/what-is-qanon.html.

Rosenfeld, Sam. *The Polarizers*. University of Chicago Press, 2017.

Sainato, Michael. "Bernie Sanders' Presidential Run Was Sabotaged by Fake News." *Observer*, November 30, 2016. https://observer.com/2016/11/bernie-sanders-presidential-run-was-sabotaged-by-fake-news/.

Salzani, Carlo. "Victimhood: Editorial Note." *dePICTions volume 4 (2024)*: *Victimhood*, Paris Institute for Critical Thinking, https://parisinstitute.org/editorial-note-iv/.

Scheler, Max. *Ressentiment*. Marquette University Press, 1994.

Setoodeh, Ramin. *Apprentice in Wonderland: How Donald Trump and Mark Burnett Took America Through the Looking Glass*. Harper, 2024.

Sitchen, Zecharia. *Genesis Revisited: Is Modern Science Catching Up With Ancient Knowledge?* Avon Books, 1990.

Smith, David. "Ron Desantis Put Nearly All His Eggs In The Basket Of A 'War On Woke.'" *The Guardian*, January 22, 2024. https://www.theguardian.com/us-news/2024/jan/21/ron-desantis-republican-presidential-candidate-dropped-out-analysis.

Smith, Marian L. "Race, Nationality, and Reality: INS Administration of Racial Provisions in U.S. Immigration and Nationality Law Since 1898." *Prologue Magazine*, Vol 34, No. 2, 2002. https://www.archives.gov/publications/prologue/2002/summer/immigration-law-1.

Smith, Peter. "Jesus Is Their Savior, Trump Is Their Candidate. Ex-president's Backers Say He Shares Faith, Values." *Associated Press*, May 18, 2024. https://apnews.com/article/trump-christian-evangelicals-conservatives-2024-election-43f25118c133170c77786daf316821c3.

Smithsonian American Art Museum. "Manifest Destiny and Indian Removal." February 2015. https://americanexperience.si.edu/wp-content/uploads/2015/02/Manifest-Destiny-and-Indian-Removal.pdf.

The Southern Poverty Law Center, "In Their Words: Hating Barack Obama." *Fighting Hate*, 2015. https://www.splcenter.org/fighting-hate/intelligence-report/2015/their-words-hating-barack-obama.

Springs, Jason A. "Zombie Nationalism: The Sexual Politics of White Evangelical Christian Nihilism." In *Religion, Populism, and Modernity: Confronting White Christian Nationalism and Racism*. Edited by Atalia Omer and Joshua Lupo. University of Notre Dame Press, 2023.

Sproul, R. C. "TULIP and Reformed Theology: Total Depravity." *Ligonier Ministries*, March 25, 2017. https://www.ligonier.org/learn/articles/tulip-and-reformed-theology-total-depravity.

Stanford University Press. "Capital and Labor." In *The American Yawp*. Accessed June 22, 2024. http://www.americanyawp.com/text/16-capital-and-labor/.

Stanley, Jason. *How Fascism Works: The Politics of Us and Them*. Random House, 2018.

Stegmaier, Werner. *What is Orientation?* DeGruyter, 2019.

Stewart, Katherine. *The Power Worshippers: Inside the Dangerous Rise of Religious Nationalism*. Bloomsbury Publishing, 2022.

Tait, Robert. "Trump Mocked For Claiming He Was 'Tortured' In Georgia Mugshot Arrest." *The Guardian*, June 25, 2024. https://www.theguardian.com/us-news/article/2024/jun/25/trump-tortured-georgia-arrest-mugshot.

Tharoor, Ishaan. "What the World's Nationalists Can Learn from Turkey and Erdogan." *Washington Post*, 26 June 2018. https://www.washingtonpost.com/news/worldviews/wp/2018/06/26/what-the-worlds-nationalists-can-learn-from-turkey-and-erdogan/.

United States Environmental Protection Agency, "The Origins of EPA." Accessed June 7, 2024. https://www.epa.gov/history/origins-epa.

The U.S. National Archives and Records Administration. "Alien and Sedition Acts (1798)." Accessed June 21, 2024. https://www.archives.gov/milestone-documents/alien-and-sedition-acts.

Velshi, Ali. "President Trump: My People Should Give Me the Attention Kim Jong Un Gets." *MSNBC*, June 15, 2018. https://www.youtube.com/watch?v=7q7SoqhCzCA.

Wade, Peter. "Trump Honored as 'Man of Decade,' Tells Crowd: 'I'm Being Indicted for You.'" *Rolling Stone*, June 25, 2023. https://www.rollingstone.com/politics/politics-news/trump-indicted-consider-it-great-badge-of-honor-1234777874/.

Wendling, Mike. "The Saga of 'Pizzagate': The Fake Story That Shows How Conspiracy Theories Spread." *BBC News*, December 2, 2016. https://www.bbc.com/news/blogs-trending-38156985.

Wikipedia. "List of Federal Political Scandals in the United States." Accessed June 7, 2024. https://en.wikipedia.org/wiki/List_of_federal_political_scandals_in_the_United_States.

Wise, Alana. "RNC votes to censure Reps. Liz Cheney and Adam Kinzinger over work with Jan. 6 panel." *NPR*, February 4, 2022. https://www.npr.org/2022/02/04/1078316505/rnc-censure-liz-cheney-adam-kinzinger-jan-6-committee-capitol.

Made in United States
North Haven, CT
23 December 2024

63389523R00085